THE ELECTRONIC BUSINESS INFORMATION SOURCEBOOK

John F. Wasik

John Wiley & Sons, Inc.
New York ▪ Chichester ▪ Brisbane ▪ Toronto ▪ Singapore

Publisher: Stephen Kippur
Editor: David Sobel
Managing Editor: Ruth Greif
Editing, Design, and Production: Publication Services

Although the author has made every effort to check the accuracy of product information such as prices, addresses, telephone numbers, and hardware requirements, this information is subject to change. The publisher therefore makes no claims for the accuracy of this information. The reader should use all product and service information solely as a guide and request current information directly from the vendor.

The author is not engaged in the rendering of online information services or consultancy. If professional advice or other expert assistance is required, the services of a competent professional should be sought.

Copyright ©1987 by John Wasik

All rights reserved. Published simultaneously in Canada.
Reproduction or translation of any part of this work beyond that permitted by Section 107 or 108 of the 1976 United States Copyright Act without the permission of the copyright owner is unlawful. Requests for permission or further information should be addressed to the Permissions Department, John Wiley & Sons, Inc.

Library of Congress Catalog-in-Publication Data

Wasik, John
    The electronic business information sourcebook.

    Bibliography: p.181
    1. Business–Data bases. 2. Business–Information services. 3. Data base searching. I. Title.
HF5548.2.W324   1987   026′.65   87-8289
ISBN 0-471-62464-0

Printed in the United States of America

87 88 10 9 8 7 6 5 4 3 2 1

ACKNOWLEDGMENTS

I wish to thank Kathleen for giving me her support and keen salesperson's insight; my brother Dan; all of the information brokers I've talked to (especially the Dallas cadre); reference librarians everywhere; and, most of all, my father and mother.

CONTENTS

TRADEMARKS AND SERVICE MARKS	viii
DATABASE SUBJECT INDEX	xiii
PREFACE	xv
CHAPTER 1 INTRODUCTION	**1**
How the Electronic Profit Center Works	4
How Databases Work	7
A Working Example: Videolog	8
What Type of Database Do I Need?	10
Where Databases Came From and Why They Are Important	11
Infocentric Success Stories	12
Specialized Databases	15
Small Business and Online Databases	16
CHAPTER 2 GETTING INFOCENTRIC	**19**
Choosing a Service	23
Infocentric Management Strategies	25
Corporate Libraries	26
Public and College Libraries	28
Information Brokers	29
An In-House Information Specialist	30
Doing the Search Yourself	32
CHAPTER 3 FRIENDLY SERVICES FOR THE BEGINNER	**37**
Telebase Systems	39
Dialog's Business Connection	42
Searchlink	44
Evaluating the Friendly Services	45

vi   THE ELECTRONIC BUSINESS INFORMATION SOURCEBOOK

CHAPTER 4	THE SOFTIES: ONLINE UTILITIES	47
	EasyLink	48
	MCI Mail	50
	The Source	51
	Compuserve	54
	Delphi	57
	BRS/BRKTHRU	58
	Dialcom	60
	Dow Jones News Retrieval	61
	NewsNet	64
CHAPTER 5	THE CORE OF THE ELECTRONIC PROFIT CENTER	67
	Dun & Bradstreet Services	68
	D&B: An Overview of Applications	73
	D&B Databases: A Special Ability	74
	Additional D&B Marketing Services	75
	Electronic Yellow Pages	76
	Instant Yellow Pages	82
CHAPTER 6	SPECIALIZED DATABASES FOR COMPANY ANALYSIS	85
	Investext: Company and Investment Information	86
	TRW Credit Reports	88
	SEC Reports Online	89
	Sales-Prospecting Databases	91
	The Sales Prospector	91
	Trade and Industry ASAP	93
	Thomas Register Online for Industrial Marketing	94
	Trinet: Detailed Company Information	96
	Sitenet	97
	VU/Text: Newspapers Online	98
	Data Times	99
CHAPTER 7	REFINED RESEARCH TOOLS	101
	Information Access Company and Data Courier: The Twin Towers	102
	IAC Specialties	103
	Knowledge Index: A Research Bargain	105
	Predicasts: Market Research Online	107
	Adtrack	109
	Mead Data Central	110
	Doing the Research: Searching Tips	114
	Doing the Search	117

CONTENTS vii

CHAPTER 8	GOVERNMENT AND TRADE SERVICES/DATABASES	121
	The TOP of the World	123
	Commerce Business Daily	126
	Pinpoint	128
	The International Business Clearinghouse and the World of Bartering/Trade	129
CHAPTER 9	ADVANCED APPLICATIONS	131
	Executive Information Systems	132
	CD-ROM: Compact Database Information	132
	E-Mail/Private Database Services	135
	ADP Automail	146
	BRS	146
	Compuserve	147
	Delphi/Grouplink	149
	GE Quick-Comm	150
	GTE Telemail	151
	Dialcom	152
	ORBIT	153
	The Source	154
	Database Applications for Retailing and Public Information	155
	Electronic Banking for Personal Computers	166
	Covidea	172
	Chase Manhattan Bank	174
	Citibank	175
	Manufacturers Hanover Trust	176
	Other Telebanking Vendors	177
	Regional Telebanking Services	178
	The Future of Telebanking	178
	The Future	180
APPENDIX A	ANNOTATED BIBLIOGRAPHY	181
APPENDIX B	INFORMATION BROKERS	183
APPENDIX C	VENDORS, SERVICES, AND TRADE GROUPS	187
APPENDIX D	SELECTED SPECIALIZED DATABASES	199
INDEX		202

TRADEMARKS AND SERVICE MARKS

The following are registered trade- or service marks used in this publication. Note: any related Dun & Bradstreet services are also trademarks of the Dun & Bradstreet Corp.

ABI/INFORM is a registered trademark of Data Courier, Inc.

ADP/Automail and *ADP/Autonet* are registered service marks of Automatic Data Processing, Inc.

Adtrack is a registered trademark of the Kingman Consulting Group, Inc.

ASCIT is a trademark of Interac Corp.

BIOSIS Previews is a registered trademark of BioSciences Information Service.

BRS/After Dark, BRS/BRKTHRU, and *BRS/Search* are registered trademarks of BRS Information Technologies, Inc.

Business Dateline is a registered trademark of Data Courier, Inc.

CLAIMS/Citation is a registered trademark of IFI/Plenum Data, Inc.

COMPENDEX is a registered trademark of Engineering Information, Inc.

Comp-U-Card is a registered trademark of Comp-U-Card International, Inc.

Compuserve is a registered trademark of Compuserve, Inc.

Comp-u-store is a trademark of Comp-U-Card International, Inc.

viii

TRADEMARKS AND SERVICE MARKS

Computer Database is a trademark of the Information Access Company.

Data Times is a registered trademark of Data Tek, Inc.

Datext is a registered trademark of Datext, Inc.

Delphi is a registered trademark of General Videotex Corp.

Dialcom is a registered trademark of Dialcom, Inc.

Dialnet, Dialog, Dialog Business Connection, and *Dialorder* are registered trademarks of Dialog Information Services, Inc., a division of the Lockheed Corporation.

Direct Access is a registered service mark of Citicorp.

Disclosure II is a registered trademark of Disclosure Information Group, Inc.

Dollars and Sense is a registered trademark of Monogram, Inc.

Donnelly Demographics is a trademark of Dun & Bradstreet Corp.

Dow Jones News Retrieval is a trademark of Dow Jones & Company, Inc.

Dun's Decision Makers, Dun's Market Identifiers, Dun's Million Dollar Directory, DunsDial, DunsPrint, DunsQuest, and *DunsVoice* are trademarks of Dun & Bradstreet Corp.

EasyLink is a registered service mark of Western Union Telegraph Co.

EasyNet is a trademark of Telebase Systems, Inc.

EasyPlex is a registered trademark of Compuserve, Inc.

ECLIPSE is a registered trademark of Mead Data Central.

Electronic Yellow Pages is a trademark of Dun & Bradstreet Corp.

Electronistore is a registered trademark of Electronistore Services, Inc.

ENERGYLINE and *ENVIRONLINE* are registered trademarks of Environment Information Center, Inc.

Excel is a registered trademark of Manufacturers Hanover Trust, Inc.

Financial Cookbook is a registered trademark of Electronic Arts, Inc.

FIND/SVP is a registered trademark of Information Clearinghouse, Inc.

FOODS ADLIBRA is a trademark of General Mills, Inc.

FYI is a registered service mark of Western Union Telegraph Co.

GEnie is a registered trademark of General Electric Corp.

Grassroots is a registered trademark of Infomart, Ltd.

Grouplink is a registered trademark of General Videotex, Inc.

Hometeller is a registered trademark of Bank of America Corp.

IBM XT is a trademark of International Business Machines Corp.

Industry Data Sources is a registered trademark of the Information Access Company.

INFO/DOC is a trademark of INFO/DOC, Inc.

InfoMaster is a registered trademark of Western Union Telegraph Co.

Infomart is a registered trademark of Infomart, Ltd.

Infonow is a registered trademark of Honeywell, Inc.

InfoPlex is a registered trademark of Compuserve, Inc.

The Information Store is a registered service mark of Information Store, Inc.

Information USA is a registered trademark of Information USA, Inc.

InfoTrac and *InfoTrac II* are trademarks of the Information Access Company.

Instant Yellow Pages is a registered trademark of American Business Lists, Inc.

Interchange is a registered trademark of Compuserve, Inc.

International Dun's Market Indentifiers is a trademark of Dun & Bradstreet Corp.

Investext is a registered trademark of the Business Research Corp.

I-Quest is a service mark of Compuserve, Inc.

Knowledge Index is a registered trademark of Dialog Information Services, a division of the Lockheed Corp.

Legal Resource Index is a registered trademark of the Information Access Company.

Lexis is a registered trademark of Mead Data Central.

LEXPAT is a registered trademark of Mead Data Central.

Lotus 1-2-3 is a registered trademark of Lotus Development Corp.

The Magazine Index is a registered trademark of the Information Access Company.

Management Contents is a registered trademark of the Information Access Company.

Mark III is a registered trademark of General Electric Corp.

MCI Mail is a registered trademark of MCI Communications, Inc.

MeadNet is a registered trademark of Mead Data Central.

Medis is a registered trademark of Mead Data Central.

Microcomputer Index is a registered trademark of Database Services, Inc.

TRADEMARKS AND SERVICE MARKS

MicroDisclosure is a registered trademark of Disclosure Information Group, Inc.

Microsoft Multiplan is a registered trademark of Microsoft, Inc.

Moneylink is a registered trademark of Monogram, Inc.

Moody's Corporate Profiles is a trademark of Dun & Bradstreet Corp.

Moody's Investors Services and *Moody's U.S. Corporate News* are trademarks of Dun & Bradstreet Corp.

National Newspaper Index is a registered trademark of the Information Access Company.

NewsFlash and *NewsNet* are registered service marks of NewsNet, Inc.

Newsearch is a registered trademark of the Information Access Company.

Nexis is a registered trademark of Mead Data Central.

Official Airline Guide is a trademark of Dun & Bradstreet Corp.

ONTYME is a registered trademark of Tymshare, Inc.

ORBIT is a registered trademark of Pergamon ORBIT Infoline, Inc.

PARTICIPATE is a trademark of Participation Systems, Inc.

Pergamon Infoline is a trademark of Pergamon ORBIT Infoline, Inc.

PFS: Plan is a registered trademark of Software Publishing, Inc.

Picture Painter NAPLPS is a registered trademark of Cableshare, Inc.

Pinpoint is a registered trademark of CACI, Inc.

Plastiserv is a registered service mark of Plastics Information Systems.

Pronto is a registered trademark of Chemical Bank, Inc.

Predicasts is a registered trademark of Predicasts, Inc.

Quick-Comm is a registered trademark of General Electric Corporation.

ReadyAccess is a trademark of Security Pacific Bank.

SalesNet is a trademark of Dun & Bradstreet Corp.

The Sales Prospector is a registered trademark of Prospector Research Services, Inc.

Shuttle is a registered trademark of Shuttle Corp.

Shuttle Scratch Pad is a registered trademark of Shuttle Corp.

The Source and *Sourcemail* are trademarks of Source Telecomputing Corp.

Spectrum is a registered trademark of Chase Manhattan Corp.

SPIN is a registered trademark of the American Institute of Physics.

Supersite is a trademark of CACI, Inc.

Symphony is a registered trademark of Lotus Development Corp.

Target is a registered trademark of Covidea, Inc.

Teleguide is a registered trademark of Infomart, Ltd.

Telenet, Telemail, and *TelemailXpress* are registered trademarks of General Telephone and Electronics, Corp.

Thomas Cook Travel USA is a trademark of Dun & Bradstreet Corp.

Thomas New Industrial Products and *Thomas Registers Online* are trademarks of Thomas Publishing Company.

Touch N' Shop is a registered trademark of Cableshare, Inc.

Touchcom is a registered trademark of Digital Techniques, Inc.

Trade and Industry ASAP is a trademark of the Information Access Company.

TRADEMARKSCAN is a registered trademark of Thomson and Thomson, Inc.

Tymnet is a registered trademark of Tymshare, Inc.

Uninet is a registered trademark of United Telecommunications, Inc.

UniPort is a registered trademark of ByVideo, Inc.

Videolog is a registered service mark of Videolog Communications Co.

VIS is a registered trademark of Tandy Corporation.

Visicalc is a registered trademark of Visicorp, Inc.

VU/Quote and *VU/Text* are registered trademarks of VU/Text Information Services, Inc., a Knight-Ridder Corp.

Ward's Business Directory is a registered trademark of the Information Access Company.

DATABASE SUBJECT INDEX

Academic-oriented research through leading trade and specialty journals and abstracts. Chapters Three, Four, and Seven.

Advertising/marketing research through Nexis and Adtrack. Chapters Six and Seven.

Banking information/applications by computer. Chapter Nine.

Bulletin boards through information services that link professionals, trade groups, and special interest groups. Chapters Four and Nine.

Business news and research, citing leading business newspapers, journals, and indexes, through Dow Jones News Retrieval, Knowledge Index, Dialog Business Connection, and other services. Chapters Three, Four, Five, Six, and Seven.

Competitive intelligence through a host of watchdog databases. Chapters Two, Three, Four, Five, Six, and Seven.

Corporate financial, management profiles. Chapters Two, Three, Four, Five, Six, and Seven.

Costs of doing information searches. It's cheaper than you think if you do it yourself. Chapter Two.

Credit reports through TRW and Dun & Bradstreet. Chapters Five and Six.

Demographic information by specific geographic areas using Donnelly Demographics and CACI databases. Chapters Four and Five.

Executive and management information. Chapters Five, Seven, and Nine.

xiii

xiv   THE ELECTRONIC BUSINESS INFORMATION SOURCEBOOK

Friendly information services for novice computer users. Chapters Three and Four.

Government business. How to do business with the government and come out ahead. Chapter Eight.

Information brokers and librarians. How you can get professionals to acquire information efficiently. Chapters Two and Three and Appendices B and C.

Information vendors, trade organizations, and services. Appendix B.

Market research through Dun & Bradstreet services, Predicasts, Nexis, Knowledge Index, and Information Access Company.

Newspapers. How to research thousands of back issues without getting newsprint on your hands. Chapter Six.

Private company information that the SEC doesn't know about. Chapters Five and Six.

Public company information that the SEC does know about. Chapters Four, Six, and Seven.

Retailing applications through databases and advanced technologies. Chapter Nine.

Sales prospecting through NewsNet, Electronic Yellow Pages, Predicasts, and Instant Yellow Pages. Chapters Five, Six, and Seven.

Research done efficiently by subject, company, SIC, location, trade names, industry group, and just about any other category. Chapters Two, Three, Five, Six, and Seven.

Specialized information, a smorgasbord of available sources. Chapters Six and Seven and Appendix D.

Utilities for computer users and information seekers. Chapter Four.

PREFACE

Information technology brings order to the chaos of information pollution and therefore gives value to data that would otherwise be useless. If users—through information utilities—can locate the information they need, they will pay for it.... This principle is the driving force behind the new electronic publishers who provide online databases ....

John Naisbitt, *Megatrends**

There is a great deal of information slumbering in computers in the form of online databases. As a journalist specializing in business, I must locate information in a short period of time and at the lowest possible cost. I nearly always find what I'm looking for in online databases, the gargantuan libraries that reside within computers. That's what led me to write this book. I wanted to share the best workshop of research tools the world has ever known—online database services.

Online databases are already hard at work in the fields of finance, law, medicine, science, engineering, and academia. Each of these areas is a formidable subject in itself, and professionals in these areas have benefited from online databases for at least a decade. Despite the general availability of this rich information resource, however, I

*Reprinted with permission. Copyright © 1982 by John Naisbitt. Warner Books, Inc.

was surprised to find that few companies or business professionals are aware of online databases. I have, therefore, chosen to focus on business and general research databases. If you should decide to venture into this area, *The Electronic Business Information Sourcebook* is a primer on online database contents and applications.

The beauty of online databases is that you don't need to know how to use a computer to take full advantage of them. I use a personal computer and online databases on a regular basis. And I'm not a programmer. I'm a journalist. If I can understand how to use them (and my background is in Psychology and English), then so can you.

I've also found that online databases and the services that accompany them save time and money. If you know how to use them, they can also help you make money.

We are in an age of *infocentrics*, which simply means that profitable businesses center around good information. Once you become infocentric, then you reap the benefits of having an *electronic profit center*—that is, a consistent producer of valuable information.

In one way, becoming infocentric means adapting to the demands of the information society. Since we are in what Harvard sociologist Daniel Bell calls a "post-industrial" age, Western society has made information its most important commodity. This development has spawned phrases like "knowledge worker" and "working smart." The online database caters to this new information culture by delivering the necessary resource (information) in an organized and efficient fashion. Online databases have thus become the most practical medium of the information age.

I wrote this book for people who need easily accessed information that is vital to their business. Whether you have a personal computer or not, you can use the electronic profit center to meet or augment your information needs.

1
INTRODUCTION

- HOW THE ELECTRONIC PROFIT CENTER WORKS
- HOW DATABASES WORK
- A WORKING EXAMPLE: VIDEOLOG
- WHAT TYPE OF DATABASE DO I NEED?
- WHERE DATABASES CAME FROM AND WHY THEY ARE IMPORTANT
- INFOCENTRIC SUCCESS STORIES
- SPECIALIZED DATABASES
- SMALL BUSINESS AND ONLINE DATABASES

The Electronic Business Information Sourcebook is a guide to finding business information. Whether you use a computer or appoint an information specialist to find the information for you, this book will tell you what valuable information is available and how best to access it. The majority of this information is contained in online databases, which are electronic libraries that can be accessed by nearly any computer user via telephone line (hence, "online"). With more than 3,000 databases available, it is impossible to detail every one of them in this volume. The *Sourcebook* therefore profiles only the databases most central to general business applications and research.

The ability to use online databases is central to creating what I call an *electronic profit center*. This unit is a managed, cost-effective device for acquiring valuable information. It isn't so much an entity as a strategy. And, as such, it will enable you to use information to your best advantage—no matter what business you are in. It will also save you time and money because it will allow you to obtain the greatest amount of information at the lowest possible cost. A well-planned electronic profit center can also help you improve your decision making by providing access to high-quality information.

Profitable businesses that thrive on good information are infocentric: information is at the center of their profit-making ability. We enhance the value of information by turning it into knowledge, which is information that is applied to a particular problem. Because our society places a high premium on value-added information, we tend to pay top dollar for the best information. Look at subscription prices for well-respected stock market newsletters. They run several hundred dollars a year. Also consider market research reports prepared by consultants, which run into the thousands of dollars. You are paying for information that, in many people's perceptions, has been transformed into valuable knowledge. And that knowledge can be profitable. But you needn't pay hundreds or thousands of dollars for valuable information.

It's no secret that a wealth of information is being stored inside computers. The problem is getting at it. Anything from our tax and checking account records to the financial figures of the largest corporations is stored in databases. A great deal of this information is accessible by the public. Online business databases are blossoming because database vendors are benefiting from a wave of newly computer-literate business people, who are using personal computers in record numbers. Of the more than eighteen million personal computers in U.S. homes and offices, a majority of those are used in business settings. Although a good portion of the business users might fall under the "administrative" category, a Stanford University study found that one in ten top corporate executives used computers daily. That's because, among its other advantages, the personal computer has smoothed many decision-making processes with spreadsheet, planning, and organizational software. And many of these computer-literate managers already regard the more than 3,000 available online databases as vital tools.

Also fueling the growth of online databases is the increasing purchase and use of the modem, a device that allows two computers to talk to each other over the telephone lines. As of this writing, about one-third of U.S. computer users owned modems. As the prices of those components steadily drop, their use is expected to grow proportionately. This growth has already translated into rich benefits for users, database vendors and *videotex* services. The largest and most successful of these services, Compuserve, has more than 250,000 users and is said to be growing at a rate of 1,000 new users (passwords) per month.

There is really nothing glamorous about making money from computers or the libraries that are contained within them, databases. The beauty of it, though, is that you don't need any computer background to understand the mechanics of online databases, nor do you need to have any sort of inclination toward machines, programming, quantum physics, or any of the other mysteries of the universe that have befuddled mankind for centuries. You may not even have time to learn about computers.

My purpose in writing this is not to make you computer-literate. You probably can't afford to spend the hours of practice required to learn all the necessary details. However, you *can* become information-literate, which, in turn, will make you infocentric. And you can become infocentric by improving your management of information.

HOW THE ELECTRONIC PROFIT CENTER WORKS

The electronic profit center is the core of your information acquisition and management strategy. Whether you have a corporate information center or a PC on your desk, you can have access to more valuable information than any "paper" source can provide. The electronic profit center is an information manager that works for you because it saves time, money, manpower, and other expensive—and limited—resources. The following list briefly summarizes some applications for your electronic profit center.

Prospecting sales leads Get names and numbers, lists and territories with speed and efficiency. Several online databases such as Electronic Yellow Pages and The Sales Prospector allow you to develop extensive mailing lists at low rates. You can target prospects by zip codes, telephone area codes, and SIC numbers.

Monitoring the competition What's their latest move? Why wait to read about it in print when it's too late? NewsNet, Industry Data Sources, Trade and Industry Index, Management Contents, Dow Jones News Retrieval, Nexis, ABI/INFORM, and other useful databases can do the monitoring automatically.

Monitoring new products What's the competition making? Has it hit the market yet? How are they marketing it? Predicasts' PTS Indexes and PROMT and others cover new products closely.

Maintaining an online library For general business research, you won't need a library card to find thousands of volumes of useful information. Online services have most libraries beat in volume of information and the sheer ease with which you can access literature.

Assisting in research and development Accelerate the R & D process. Bypass paper libraries, consultants, and market researchers by selecting information from online databases.

Monitoring trade journals and newsletters A good system can find out invaluable trade reports before they hit print. Through NewsNet, ABI/INFORM, Trade and Industry Index, and others, you can find publications not available in most libraries. You and your company can save on the exorbitant subscription fees of most newsletters.

Researching mergers and acquisitions Identify potential takeover or merger targets through extensive online research. While you call the shots, an online database can provide the initial research at a lower cost than an investment banking service could offer. Corporate raider T. Boone Pickens reportedly uses online databases to scout his quarry.

Online consulting Why pay a consultant an exorbitant fee to do research when you can do it yourself? By using online services such as PTS/Prompt, Frost & Sullivan, Adtrack, and FIND/SVP, you can tap into a plethora of industry-specific market research.

Researching demographics and exploring new territory
Identify and exploit new, fertile markets for your product or service. Compuserve's CACI Supersite databases

and Donnelly demographic and marketing databases could serve your company at a fraction of the cost a consultant or market research firm would demand. These databases also provide detailed demographic profiles.

Telemarketing Let an online database select and refine telephone lists and prospects. The Electronic Yellow Pages, Instant Yellow Pages, and Dun & Bradstreet services can produce highly refined lists.

Providing mailman, courier, and messenger services Send electronic mail, a telex, or any other message anywhere. Western Union's EasyLink, MCI Mail, Dialcom, Compuserve, and The Source are information specialists that provide a full range of communications services from telex to electronic mail. These services save time and money over express mail and courier services.

Overseas marketing Identify and seize opportunities in foreign markets. Databases that use key government trade information from Commerce Department Trade Opportunities, Foreign Trader Indexes, and Commerce Business Daily give you overseas sales leads and trade opportunities.

Delivering documents Order and move documents through your computer. Most information brokers not only get you the documents you need, but can research for you as well.

Monitoring government regulations Keep an eye on the latest rules and regulations from the agencies and Congress. Taxes and business laws merit special coverage.

Providing economics advice An online database is a bountiful source of knowledge on economic matters. Dow Jones, Dialog, and Compuserve provide a wealth of economic data.

Networking Through bulletin boards on The Source, Compuserve, and Delphi, you can get in touch with colleagues in your profession or business to swap ideas and make new contacts.

HOW DATABASES WORK

It may be true that only God can make a tree, but nearly any thinking person can understand and/or construct a database. As far as concepts go, a database is hardly up there with artificial intelligence or high-energy particle physics. The underlying principles of databases are logic and form. A well-constructed database can work well for many people. In the process of becoming infocentric, it is therefore important to understand how a database is structured.

Consider the building of a home. It starts out with the naked land, under which an infrastructure is built. That includes sewer lines, water mains, and gas, electric, and telephone lines. From there, the builder either digs a basement and pours a concrete foundation or pours a slab. Then the frame goes up, the roof goes on, the walls are assembled, and everything else follows from insulation to lighting fixtures. Although databases are treehouses compared to the modern three-bedroom ranch, it's the structure that counts.

Databases start with raw data as the most basic components of their infrastructures. Data are then channeled into a framework, which, for our purposes, is the database structure. What holds the rest of this house together is a frame of indexes (or menus) that separate many rooms of pages.

In order to get into the indexes or menus, you must first get into the system by logging on (or ringing the doorbell and having the system let you in). Once inside, you choose your index/menu or take another route and use the faithful staff of butlers called *keywords* or search languages.

Keywords will allow you to bypass the indexes, which serve as anterooms to bigger rooms of information. They also serve as light switches that instantly illuminate certain parts of the database.

Keywords save you time because they can match the subject you are interested in. If you want information on General Motors, for instance, one keyword called "GM" could get you there as fast as your system would allow.

You can also find information in the database by using a search language that may employ *parametric* searching. This database tool allows you to look for information by using more than one word in a phrase. A parametric search will turn up a number of words or phrases that resemble what you want. Say you want to find a company report on a company named ABC. Is it ABC, Inc.; Company; or Limited? A parametric search will give you all the combinations. You can be inexact and still find what you want. Say you also wanted to locate information on GM's marketing strategy. You would ask the system for "GM" and "marketing strategy." This method uses what industry people call *Boolean* connectors like "and," "or," and "not." This way makes your search more "powerful." That's computer talk for more efficient. It also enables you to narrow or expand your search.

Since we are building a house that is in harmony with nature, the entire database is structured like a tree. You build a database tree with several roots and limbs, where each limb is an index and each piece of information a leaf.

A WORKING EXAMPLE: VIDEOLOG

Many vendors that sell online databases are actually charging you rent (for "connect time") to enter a system that will guide you to one or all of the databases. Because the vendors have spent millions on the best software to allow you to access the databases, they claim to have "user-friendly systems," or systems that require no prior preparation or disclaimers. For the novice, these systems are anything but friendly. For the experienced user, they are a bit more manageable.

Of the more successful purely business online systems, Videolog is one those rare applications of online technology that found almost immediate widespread acceptance.

In October, 1984, Videolog began serving the electronic components market. Its parent, Videolog Communications, had done its homework in determining that engineers needed an up-to-date catalog on semiconductors and related devices. The paper catalogs were constantly out of date and cumbersome, and they had pricing information that fluctuated with rapidly changing market conditions. Videolog and its market seemed right for each other.

To date, Videolog serves more than 1,000 companies in the U.S., Canada, Japan, and the Middle East. It is an international online catalog that uses the same telephone network as Compuserve. At the core of the service are selection guides covering 500,000 components from more than 700 suppliers. It also lists a directory of more than 14,000 industry sources.

Backed by Capital Cities Communications Corp. and the Schweber family, Videolog gained immediate recognition from companies providing the information and those using it. Electronics engineers relied upon Videolog to supply them with component descriptions, suppliers, secondary sources, and, in some cases, illustrations that employ graphics.

In addition to the catalog section, Videolog offers electronic mail, the *Harris Who's Who in the Electronics Industry, Datatek* pricing guides, news items from *Electronics News* (7–13 frames from Monday's edition), and new product listings.

The service gains its revenues from users, who pay anywhere from $15 an hour to $25 an hour to access it, and the manufacturers who pay to place their information in the system. The pricing is typical of nearly all videotex and online database systems. You pay for the right to use a telephone network and the time you spend talking to a computer.

What makes Videolog a genuine business-to-business service is its ability to search through thousands of frames of information for one specific part. After you log on, Videolog's menu offers choices of component directory, product/service directory, company directory, product news, communications services, industry calendar, and news from Videolog.

Searches can be performed by entering a product name or class, a company, or other specific parameters. Videolog employs parametric and keyword searching to find parts. Those search methods involve specifying a range of variables in a category. For example, a user who wants to find a "16 K UV EPROM chip" can find it by specifying a manufacturer or other variables. A parametric search will indicate when it has found the several thousand parts that fit the general specifications of the search request. The user can then chose to see what's listed or ask for more clearly defined specifications such as part, part type, or root number.

Videolog illustrates how thousands of users in different locations at different times can access the system—at their own convenience and with little prior training. In this respect, videotex and online databases place information seekers in McLuhan's "Global Village," where the cost of the information is related more to the cost of delivery (telecommunications) than the original production cost of the information.

WHAT TYPE OF DATABASE DO I NEED?

There are many types of databases. Principally, any collection of information, or data, stored in a computer in a structured, organized way, is a database. There are, however, subtle distinctions among databases. Most companies have what are called internal databases, or information that can be accessed only by people inside the company. They are administered by database management systems (DBMS) and are not to be confused with external online databases, which are generally accessible to the public by telephone lines, modems, and computers. Most large public libraries have access to online databases. Internal databases, for the most part, are off limits to all but a select few.

The kinds of databases described in this book include: (1) *full-text* databases, in which an entire article is available; (2) *bibliographic* databases, in which articles are summarized in citations or abstracts; (3) *numeric* databases, containing a lot of numbers; and (4) *listings* of names and addresses. There are also databases whose sole province is scientific and technical information. Services like Nexis provide full-text articles, while Dialog offers mostly bibliographic and numeric databases. In terms of time savings, reading an abstract is better than reading full text. However, when you want the maximum amount of information, full text is superior.

To select the database or service you need, decide upon your application first. Are you looking for sales leads, marketing research, or demographic information? Online databases can be extremely specialized or contain a broad range of information. When you choose your application, you should either (1) approach a librarian with online database search capabilities or an information broker (see Chapter Two), or (2) train yourself to perform your own information search (see Chapter Three on "friendly" services).

WHERE DATABASES CAME FROM AND WHY THEY ARE IMPORTANT

Online databases have been around ever since the early days of the space program. One of the children of the space race, the online database was first used by scientists and technicians. The largest of these baby boomers was the online service, Dialog, originally created by the Lockheed Corporation to serve the needs of the space program. Although it was once the exclusive domain of engineers, Dialog has become the behemoth of the business information industry, laying claim to the largest service of its type and the one preferred by many librarians and information brokers.

Using online databases to deliver current, crucial information to businesses is neither a new idea nor a unique one. Some top database vendors, such as Dow Jones News Retrieval, have been around for ten years. While companies like Dow Jones have been marketing their product to very specific audiences such as the Fortune 500, the applications of online databases for more specialized businesses and niche markets are just beginning to be developed.

The costs of using online databases vary widely. Generally, you pay for telecommunications (telephone) charges and "connect" time. There also are additional charges for memberships, software, and fees for information brokers if you decide to use them. Expect to pay anywhere from $6 to $150 an hour for connect and telecommunications. The more specialized the database, the more you'll pay. Brokers will charge you for the costs of getting the information in addition to an hourly or flat rate for their time.

INFOCENTRIC SUCCESS STORIES

The kinds of people who have benefited from online information provided by computer information services come from all professions, from large corporations and small firms. And they probably have little or no computer background. A great deal of the critical information they've found is stored in online databases, where they can be tapped by the public—usually at a nominal cost twenty-four hours a day.

The testimonials are legion, as the following examples show:

- Cincinnati Time started a direct-mail campaign using 60,000 prospects from Dun's Marketing that targeted fourteen service areas by SIC code, number of employees, individual name and title, and geography. The campaign led to a four percent response rate with a conversion rate of leads to sales of thirty to forty percent. A CT product manager estimates that the direct-mail campaign boosted sales twenty-five percent in the fourth quarter of 1984.
- A heavy machinery company executive from a Chicago suburb looking for overseas end-users of rebuilt engines went to the Commerce Department's database searcher in Chicago. A few days later, he had a list of 200 companies that were prospects for his products.
- Shearson Lehman/American Express needed a prospecting system for a new executive services group that would cater to clients with portfolios that began at $100,000. By using the Dun's Market Identifiers database, the group achieved high conversion rates from prospects to clients—"the best in the business," according to a Shearson sales manager.
- A sales representative for Mead Data Central, which produces the Nexis and Lexis services, was looking for sales leads in a specific geographic area. By using a feature in Nexis that will track a press release by telephone area code, he came up with a list of companies within an area code in a matter of minutes.
- Nonbusiness professionals have also discovered the benefits of instant information. Dr. Glenn Tisman of Whittier, California, had a patient who was bleeding in the intensive care unit of a local hospital. It was around midnight, and the hospital called him at home. His patient, according to his recollection, had "postsurgical bleeding problems that, according to the current literature, were not readily manageable. The patient

was given the usual blood products to try to stop the bleeding, but this was not successful."

Since the hospital's medical library was closed, Dr. Tisman turned to another resource, his Apple computer, which he had at home. Searching through Dialog and another specialty database called Medline, he found nineteen different abstracts, which he promptly downloaded into his computer. One of the articles that turned up in his search described a new blood replacement product that he had not known about. Immediately, he phoned the hospital, recommending the new treatment. On his rounds later that morning, he was pleased to find that his patient's bleeding had stopped. He credits the article from the literature search with saving her life.

- A policeman was attempting to track down a truck that had been involved in a hit-and-run accident. The only lead the policeman had was the name on the side of the truck, but no license plate number. A search of Dun's Market Identifiers revealed not only the name of the company, but the location of the firm. The case was closed shortly thereafter.
- General Electric uses online databases such as Nexis and Dialog for competitive analysis. They look at the strategies of competitors, press coverage, new product development, and manufacturing site divestitures.
- The use of the online service Nexis helped an insurance company more accurately quote on a policy covering the construction of a sewer system in Cairo, Egypt. By researching various risks through Nexis, the insurance company was able to raise a broker's quote from two million to seventeen million dollars.
- Norman Plagge, a vice-president of The Northern Trust Company, uses a variety of online services to retrieve information and save time. He and his staff use the services to do anything from finding timely information relating to a marketing strategy in the People's Repub-

lic of China to getting information on customers and prospects.
- An electrical manufacturer uses online databases for surveying competitors' strategies, R & D spending, and trademarks and monitoring the trade and technical press.
- A major New York state defense contractor uses database research to analyze his competition and to study government regulations, possible joint-venture partners, and backgrounds on individuals in the industry.
- An insurance company in New York prepares briefing books for traveling executives that summarize the places they will visit. The information is gleaned from online databases.
- A major oil company uses online databases to track developments in parts of the world where they have investments or are considering new operations.

SPECIALIZED DATABASES

Although databases may cater to nearly any general business research need, they can also become extremely specialized. For example, take the complicated business of federal contracting. Those companies that want to do business with the government but are not already involved ordinarily face a mindset that says, "Only those firms that have political connections get the contracts." Not so, thanks to the computerization of some key government databases and firms that specialize in distributing the information.

Thalia Gerachis of American Management Systems, Inc., a software system designer, does business with the government in a classic infocentric way. Gerachis's company uses a service called CBD Online, which is an electronic version of *Commerce Business Daily*. For businesses that contract with the federal government, CBD is their bible. It lists requests for proposals (RFPs) for contracts and catalogs government-related business opportunities.

CBD Online will list all the contents in the print version of the journal. One of its unique features is the ability to program the system to list RFPs according to a specific industry. Gerachis says that she reads through CBD Online "the first thing in the morning when I pour my coffee."

"It (CBD Online) shows me what's out there. It also has a service to show you who won a contract in the past. They have a way of containing information that I can't physically hold."

American Management Systems employs the most fundamental rule of infocentric management. Technology has not only made information more manageable, but is also able to deliver it efficiently and lower the cost of doing business for those who use the service.

Another outgrowth of the dramatic rise of infocentricity has been the broader range of information services made available to businesses. Companies now seem less willing to use the services of traditional consultants, lawyers, accountants, and market researchers, preferring instead to do their own research or hire information brokers. The whole corporate information base is changing because of the shift to internal research with online databases. And those who have the right information have more clout in the marketplace.

SMALL BUSINESS AND ONLINE DATABASES

Kathleen Kennedy, a Dallas-based information broker, can easily illustrate the growing sophistication of corporate information needs. Like many independent information brokers, Kennedy has a specialty, which is generating labor market reports for outplacement firms. She notes that her clients are willing to "pay whatever it takes" to find certain information.

A typical request for her service involved a real estate developer working on a building complex. A company that wanted to cater to insurance companies needed to know before they broke ground how many insurance companies there were in the area in which they were building. Kennedy ran a search of Electronic Yellow Pages, which gave her listings of insurance companies in a given area, and the job was completed.

One of Kennedy's clients (not the one involved in the previous example) can attribute some new business to Kennedy's infocentric skills. As a microcomputer systems consultant, Lynn Gilfillan relies upon Kennedy's market research to determine what's available in the thousands of software and hardware packages on the market. When Gilfillan gets a contract to place a microcomputer system in a small business, she turns to Kennedy to search software databases and generate lists for appropriate applications programs. From there, Gilfillan can prepare a feasibility report for her client on what software to buy.

Because it is virtually impossible for any individual to keep track of all the new products in the computer marketplace, Kennedy's service is an "extraordinarily cost-effective one," Gilfillan said. In turn, Gilfillan can offer her clients "a very comprehensive service so that they can make an informed decision."

The relationship between an infocentric manager and the information itself needn't be a direct one, as the previous case proves. But knowing what services and information are available can make the difference between wasting money on traditional methods or building an efficient electronic profit center.

2
GETTING INFOCENTRIC

- CHOOSING A SERVICE
- INFOCENTRIC MANAGEMENT STRATEGIES
- CORPORATE LIBRARIES
- PUBLIC AND COLLEGE LIBRARIES
- INFORMATION BROKERS
- AN IN-HOUSE INFORMATION SPECIALIST
- DOING THE SEARCH YOURSELF

Before you begin searching for the information you need, you should ask yourself a few questions. The following are a few basic considerations that should start your information checklist.

Availability Is the information I need available in print form for free or at a reasonable price? Can I pick up the information *when* I need it at a library, or do I have to wait several weeks to order it?

Time factors How soon do I need the information? How much time will it take a person in my company to get the information? How soon can an outside information specialist get it?

Cost Will the cost of getting the information exceed its worth? Will the cost of the information mean the difference between getting a sale, landing an account, or attracting new business? Will it be cheaper to order the information through an information service or send an employee to a library and spend several hours locating and copying what I need? This is the most variable factor.

The elegance of using online databases is that you do not need to know that much about computers to know how to acquire valuable information. Chances are, if you don't have a computer and a modem, you won't need them anyway. Whether you have them or not, you are now ready to begin calculating your need for online information.

You need to know what type of information can be accessed *only* by computers. Some of the information in this book is available in print form as well; however, it could be less expensive to get it from a computer database search.

There is a great deal of research that supports the cost-benefit relationship of using online databases versus "manual" searching, or sending out a worker to a library to pore over stacks of reference material.

In a 1975 survey of online database users done by

Wanger, Cuadra, and Fishburn, the researchers found that nearly ninety-two percent of managers queried responded that "all or most of the anticipated benefits had been realized." Additionally, the study found that seventy-two percent of the managers realized a faster turnaround time (in information acquisition), sixty-eight percent gained access to additional sources of information, and fifty-seven percent reduced their staff time (in information retrieval).

The main benefit of online searching as opposed to conventional methods is increased productivity. That is, those who need the information spend less time looking for it. Consequently, they have more time to spend on other activities.

In terms of cost per search, the savings become even more significant. Studies performed between 1974 and 1978 on online usage in the government and private sector showed that online searches cost from $25 to $85 per search, compared to up to $250 for manual searches. The studies also showed that online database usage saved a great deal of time for the searchers. Average online search times ranged from 27 to 150 minutes; from 60 minutes to 22 hours for manual searches.

Of course, if you choose to do online searching yourself, you or your business must be prepared for a highly variable set of costs. The "in-house" scenario must include a computer, modem, telephone line, a trained research staffer and all accompanying labor, maintenance, photocopying, and other processing costs. In order to do in-house searching, you and your staff need some familiarity with using computers, as well.

How do you decide when to use in-house resources or to go for outside help and employ a special librarian or information broker? The following guidelines based on studies done by King Research, Rockville, Md., should be helpful:

Use a broker if you perform 60 searches or less.

Use manual searches or use public or academic libraries if you need from 61 to 200 searches.

Use manual and online searches if you need from 201 to 6,595 searches.

Use manual and in-house online computer searches if you need to perform more than 6,595 searches.

As a footnote to these numbers, you should realize that the study was not meant to be a recommendation to businesses and was based on conservative, fixed costs of $6,325. The numbers are for comparison purposes only. Your fixed costs will vary tremendously depending on the equipment available (or your need to purchase it), training, manuals, and other necessary items. One point is clear, though. For a heavy volume of searches, it pays to have in-house online searching. Using brokers may be more cost-effective if you require smaller numbers of searches. But these are purely economic considerations.

How do you determine what is a heavy volume of searching? First, you'll have to look at your own information needs, read through the chapters in this book relevant to you, and determine if the information you need can be found in online databases. For example, companies or individuals that need sales and profit numbers on companies on a daily basis will find that such information is most efficiently provided by online databases.

A heavy volume of database searching would involve anywhere from ten searches per day on up. Broadly defined, one search equals one inquiry into a database for one set of facts. If you need to do 25 searches per day, that's 6,500 searches per year, based on a 260-day (5-day-week) year. That's generally considered to be a high volume of searches. Before you make a decision on researching in-house or brokering your searches, you can make your info-centric strategy even more effective by developing a working knowledge of the costs of using online databases.

CHOOSING A SERVICE

While we're on the subject of costs, if you've already invested in a personal computer, a modem, and communications software, the next basic cost is for your online service(s). If you don't have access to a computer, read on.

Nearly all the services charge by the hour. Some charges range from $6 to $160 an hour, depending on the information. Most have electronic mail and article- or document-ordering services, which usually involve additional cost.

This delivery is expensive compared to, say, photocopying something at a library, but keep in mind that you are paying a premium to have relatively hard-to-find material delivered to you in a short period of time. Here is a checklist when considering online service costs (for computer users):

Start-up, initiation, or subscription fee This could range from $40 to $65. In terms of your overall costs, this will be a minor consideration.

Monthly minimum Because there is no way to tell how much you will be using the service at first, take a close look at the information the service provides. Monthly minimums are for the big users.

Connect charges This will be your greatest expense. A host of services give you *some* free connect time, but even then your costs will be considerable. You can gauge your information costs by means of a trial usage period. Will you use the service once a day or only once a month? Estimate your monthly charges from here. You can count on saving money, however, if you take advantage of the services that cut their rates at nights and on the weekends. Some examples: Knowledge Index, BRS/After Dark, Compuserve.

Telecommunications charges This is the cost you will incur for telephone time, which some services include in their hourly rate. This, too, should be taken into consideration when choosing a service. Most services have their own low-cost networks. Some have toll-free numbers.

Training For database vendors like Dialog, you need training before you go online. That will cost $165 for a daily session. It's worth it. The more specialized or involved a service gets, the more you need training. Dialog is, however, in the minority. You don't need training for The Source, Compuserve, Knowledge Index, or any other service targeted to "home" users. Also, Dialog Business Connection doesn't require training and is relatively easy to use. Services like Mead Data Central's Nexis and Lexis provide free classes.

Manuals Again, some databases require that you use the manuals to get the most for your money. These range in price from $50 on down. Most of the smaller services give you a user guide for nothing. Not all manuals are helpful, though. Some of the books mentioned in the bibliography of this book might be more useful.

Ordering articles, abstracts, offline prints This is a relatively expensive service that you can perform while you are on the system. Offline prints that are ordered and mailed to you average around $10 each. It's highly worthwhile if you need the information quickly. If you need it immediately, you can print it online, which can be even more expensive, since the meter's always running after you log on. Most of the time it's cheaper to read the abstracts, take down the information, and have a librarian track down what you want. But you can do that only with periodicals that a library has on the shelves. If your information is hard to find—like some newsletters or trade papers—offline or online printing may be the only way you will get what you want.

Remember, this evaluation requires that you judge how much your time and the information you need are worth. If you don't use a computer, remember that you can get others to gather the information for you. The key to infocentric management is knowing what information is there for you. Accessing it becomes a minor factor once you know what you're looking for.

An electronic profit center will more than pay for itself if you use it often; however, if you feel that the costs would be excessive or that your working environment is not suited to online searching, then consider seeking outside help. The information that I will introduce in the following sections is designed to help you streamline your information-gathering process, regardless of the size of your operation or the strategy you choose to pursue.

INFOCENTRIC MANAGEMENT STRATEGIES

There are three options available to you in your infocentric management strategy:

1. Go to an information research professional.
2. Appoint or hire (then train) an information specialist within your company.
3. Search the services yourself.

Each option has its advantages and disadvantages.

With the exception of public or corporate librarians, information research professionals are either members of large research or consulting houses or independent information brokers. Whichever you choose, you can generally count on dealing with well-trained personnel, able to conduct full-service operations. The main advantage in using information research professionals is that they already know their territory. Some even specialize in particular areas and databases. Because of their expertise, they can save you time and acquire information far more efficiently than start-up, in-house operations.

One drawback, however, is that you will pay much more than you would if you had decided to consult a public or corporate librarian and a huge amount more than if you or someone in your company could do the research single-handedly. According to King Research, broker costs average about $100, although that figure depends on what's being searched, how long it takes, and what additional costs may be involved, such as document delivery, photocopying, and royalty charges. Information brokering, it should be noted, is still a premium service. Additionally, information specialists may provide a slower turnaround time than would an in-house operation, and, by using an intermediary, you would be more removed from the information.

In the remainder of the chapter, I will deal in greater detail with the various options available to you in your infocentric management strategy. But no matter who does your information search, you will need to know what information is available. Since this volume is written for any level of information seeker, I'll describe a few services that you might want to try on your own. If you can't afford the time or if you don't have a computer, it's a simple matter for brokers or librarians to search them for you. Even if you decide to do your searches yourself, talk to a librarian who knows online research. It could save a lot of time.

CORPORATE LIBRARIES

I like librarians. To me, they are the greatest humanitarians in the world. Why? Because I've always believed it was timely information and education that raised people above poverty and oppression. And librarians are the caretakers of that knowledge. They shepherd it skillfully into our minds. A good librarian can get you to information faster than anyone. Unlike tipsters, their information is reliable and verifiable. They save you time and can help you make money.

One of the greatest resources your company may have is a corporate library. The larger companies have them. The more progressive, infocentric companies have access to online databases and may have professionals available to search them for you in an *information center*. An information center is a tremendous resource because you don't have to leave your corporate environment to get what you need. The information is also easily accessible—especially if your company library has a sizable budget.

Most well-stocked corporate libraries will subscribe to:

Dialog A database vendor that is a supplier of more than 200 databases.

Mead Data Central Once solely a paper-products company, Mead Data Central produces three services called Lexis (primarily for legal research), Nexis (for business), and Medis (for medical research). All three have solid reputations in the information business.

BRS These initials stand for Bibliographic Retrieval Service, which supplies a host of business research services in its Search, BRKTHRU, and After Dark utilities.

Dow Jones News Retrieval Owned and operated by the producers of the *Wall Street Journal* and *Barron's,* DJNRS is the sine qua non source for current business/investment news and background.

NewsNet A smaller, though detailed service that specializes in newsletters, news, TRW credit reports, and a smorgasbord of useful business information services.

Your first step is to ask your librarian which of these

services your company subscribes to and how to search them. There are other services, but they probably won't be as useful to you as the aforementioned ones. These services provide a lion's share of nonfinancial business information. Acquiring them and training a librarian to use them is one of the first moves in becoming infocentric. Once you know what these databases contain, you can converse with your librarian more efficiently. The following chapters will fill you in on the details.

PUBLIC AND COLLEGE LIBRARIES

One of the greatest almost-kept secrets is the booty of information that can be obtained for almost nothing from a local or college library.

Unlike corporate libraries, which vary in capabilities in direct proportion to the size of the company, public and academic libraries have long had access to online databases. The most wonderful thing about them is that not only are they well staffed (in most larger libraries) and up to date, but they also have a staff of people who may specialize in online searching.

For example, the central Chicago library has one of the finest, most professional computer-assisted search centers (as do other large, metropolitan libraries) in the Midwest. They not only have the above-named services but they also have expertise in catering to business people. One librarian, Kathleen Prendergast, wasn't afraid to tell me when I came searching for information that I shouldn't waste my money on online database searches that were more cheaply accomplished by scanning print sources.

You should be aware that in public or academic libraries you might have to wait a few days for an information search to be completed, and few, if any, libraries will deliver the search results to you. But that's not necessarily a drawback. Their knowledge is a visible asset to your business, especially considering the cost, which may be subsidized by your taxes.

Academic libraries tend to perform more specialized searches. Technical or scientific literature searches are more popular in the ivory towers. On the whole, college libraries also will favor students and professors, although many do work for the general public.

Suburban libraries, depending upon the wealth of the local library taxing district, may not have the resources of a city library, although I've discovered some surprisingly complete business information centers in suburban libraries. Generally, the larger the community and the more business concentrated in it, the better your chances of finding online services.

INFORMATION BROKERS

Like all services that you pay for, brokers will charge you more for what you don't know than for what you do. But they can also save you money by doing a database search professionally and within cost limits. Information brokers range from full-service houses that focus on consulting, information retrieval, and document delivery, to the independents, who might be specialists in information retrieval in a particular subject.

I've dealt with both the big and the small. As far as personalized service goes, you can't beat the independents. They not only take great care in seeing that you get what you need, but they are also thorough. Many are former librarians. They know their trade.

The larger information brokerages might want to sell you a survey or get you on a $6,000 retainer. Several have deposit accounts for large clients with volume orders. Or they might have a wealth of information already on tap, gathered from the surveys they've already done. Besides the sheer numbers of true experts they can put on your request, they know the information business well. More than likely, they have some of the top businesses in a given industry as their clients. In other words, they take the corporate team approach as opposed to the entrepreneurial approach of the independents. You will probably pay more for their services than for those of the smaller firms. Both concerns will process, gather, and deliver what you need.

Keep in mind that nearly everything an information broker does, you or your in-house information specialist can do for much less if you are set up correctly. But that's not to say that a broker can't do the job more cost effectively. It depends on the job, the broker's expertise, and the subject.

For a list of recommended information brokers, please turn to Appendix B.

AN IN-HOUSE INFORMATION SPECIALIST

The next best thing to doing it yourself is having someone in the office do it for you. So, after you have determined your information needs, it's best to appoint someone in your office whom you would like to have as an information specialist. Chances are, you won't need to hire a new employee to be your specialist. People in corporate environments deal with enormous amounts of information every day.

The type of person best suited to the job of information specialist should have some reference, research, or library background. Information specialists must know the basics of corporate research and be intelligent, flexible, and inquiring. The best positions from which to choose candidates would be:

> Administrative Assistant
> Clerk
> Expediter
> Word-Processing Typist
> Departmental Assistant
> Researcher

Clearly, and most importantly, your information specialist should be comfortable with and trained in the use of a personal computer. I don't recommend using secretaries because it is important that they not be distracted by phone calls; short, demanding assignments; or reception-related tasks. Secretaries can do the job, however, on a part-time basis where needed.

Your chosen information specialist will, of course, need not only your guidance but also—like yourself—good training, which is provided by the majority of the services. Training for your specialist is crucial. Your specialist should have outside training by the database vendors once you have selected them. But you will also need to review carefully the offerings of the various online services first, obtain subscriptions and manuals from them, and make sure that the services you choose will train your specialist properly.

Once you have chosen an information specialist, you will need to designate a special work area to provide the necessary space for a personal computer, a printer, a telephone and modem, manuals, and plenty of workspace. The personal computer you choose is up to you. If it's compatible with the software that the database services will accept, then it will do.

As far as compensation is concerned, you may consider some salary adjustment due to the more specialized nature of the position. An information specialist is not simply processing paper or documents anymore. The more information-intensive corporations have whole departments of information specialists. Think of your specialist as an extension of your office: the marketing research department, research and development, public relations, and competitive intelligence. This person could be more valuable to you than any other administrator.

In appointing an information specialist, then, you are delegating a person to streamline, massage, and discipline an unruly information flow into your electronic profit center. It's like hiring a consultant to improve your business, except that you're paying a lot less for a lot more service that's delivered on a consistent and timely basis.

DOING THE SEARCH YOURSELF

This is an introductory section for present computer users. For more detailed information, consult some of the books listed in the bibliography. If you don't want to do your own searching, skip this section.

Computer novices take note. You don't need to have a degree in computer science to be able to search online databases. If you know how to dial into an online service using a modem, that's a good starting point. The rest is a constant education process.

If you choose the pioneer approach, you should be familiar with the necessary equipment that will help you reach your goal of becoming infocentric. You don't need an elaborate set-up to begin accessing online databases, but it would help if you started with a personal computer and a modem. Any computer from an inexpensive Commodore to an IBM XT will do pretty much the same job. A modem, however, is a more particular matter. The modem is the device by which your computer can converse with another computer. It takes data, turns them into beeps, and transmits them along a telephone line. The rate at which it sends or receives is bits per second or *baud*.

Modems vary in price from $40 on up. It pays to invest in a good one, because it will do the bulk of the communicating and make your life a lot easier. Desirable features are auto-answer and dial functions in an asynchronous mode. All modern modems on the market are at least 300 baud with the more expensive models at 1,200 and 2,400 baud. You can go as fast as 9,600 baud. These units are currently the Porsches of the industry. Although you get the most for your money at a higher baud rate (because the information can be received faster), many online services charge higher rates for 1,200- and 2,400-baud access.

Communications Software

No initial set-up is complete without communications software. The software tells the modem how to communicate; it's the translator for a very high-paced conversation. Several modems come "bundled" with software. If the modems don't come with the software, then you need to buy the software before you can begin. For some "dumb" terminals, though, you may not need software, because a dumb terminal may not have any processing power. You really don't need software for searching online databases—unless you want to store to disk. That's primarily what software will do for you. It can do everything from automatically dialing a service to storing files.

Several services such as Dow Jones and Compuserve have software specially made for them. Some modem/software packages have discount coupons for free services, so it pays to shop around. Remember to buy software that is tailored for your system. Some first-time users forget that IBM-compatible programs won't run on an Apple, and so forth.

Going Online

You are almost ready to settle down with that cup of coffee and go on line. But there are a few things to remember first. When you turn on your computer and "boot it up," you'll need to make sure that the communications *parameters* on the software match the service you are accessing. Parameters, which take less than a minute to set, are the technical requirements that ensure that your computer and the computer you are calling are talking the same dialect. The word *configuration* is also used to mean *parameters*. I think *configuration* is used by computer makers west of the Mississippi. In any case, configuration and parameters are identical in meaning. The most important thing to remember is that you want to match your parameters with that of the service you will be signing onto as you prepare to communicate.

34 THE ELECTRONIC BUSINESS INFORMATION SOURCEBOOK

After you boot up, you will have a choice of settings:

Parity A choice of even, odd, or none. This is a way of encoding characters. A wrong choice could give you a garbled transmission.

Synchronous Not usually in your parameters menu, but you should make sure you have an asynchronous modem. The vast majority of modems for personal computers are, so this is not a major decision.

Duplex A choice of full or half. A full duplex setting allows your computer to have a two-way conversation with the online service. Half is a bit lonelier.

Speed A choice of 300 to 9,600 baud, which translates to the number of characters per second that the modem sends across telephone lines. Note that many services charge a premium rate for 1,200 baud and up, although, in the long run, you can save money because of the increased volume of transmitted information. A few services can take 2,400 baud.

Stop bits A choice of one or two. More conversational instructions.

Data bits A choice of seven or eight. Another important parameter.

Line feed A choice of no LF, or CR (carriage return) and LF. Tells the computer when to start a new line of information.

Pulse or touch-tone Allows you to communicate in only one mode. There may also be a switch on your telephone. Be sure to check it.

Auto-dial Not a communications parameter, but a key, time-saving option your modem and software may have. If you have auto-dial, you can program your modem to dial for you. This is not a feature on acoustic modems, where you actually have to put the handset in a cradle. A direct-connect modem is preferable to an acoustic since the direct model eliminates outside noise. Telephone line noise is another problem, as you will discover.

Dialing up the Online Service

Although most online services will provide you with either an 800 or a local number, it's best to make sure that you are dialing a low-cost exchange. Long distance can be a killer on a data line since, when you are talking on a computer, you tend to lose track of the length of a connection. It's possible to rack up some really hefty charges and not even be aware of it.

Most services provide you with a local Telenet, Tymnet, or other network number. Dialog and Mead Data Central have their own networks, called Dialnet and Meadnet respectively. These numbers hook into what is called a *packet-switching* network, so you are billed only for a local call even if the host computer of the service you are calling is on the other side of the continent. The instructions for dialing into the services couldn't be simpler.

Once you dial into a system, you'll need a log-on and a password, which the database services provide to you. The rest is up to you.

3
FRIENDLY SERVICES FOR THE BEGINNER

- TELEBASE SYSTEMS
- DIALOG'S BUSINESS CONNECTION
- SEARCHLINK
- EVALUATING THE FRIENDLY SERVICES

In the early days of online databases, it could truly be said that there was no such thing as a "user-friendly" online database or information utility. But, as the database vendors began to orient themselves more and more to nonexpert microcomputer end-users, online databases became more and more easy to use.

In the last five years, something of a revolution has been taking place in the design of interfaces for online databases. (Interfaces, in this regard, are the software tools that connect users with databases.) Many of the databases maintained by Dialog and other vendors can be searched only by someone with several months of training. Nonexpert users therefore needed a "painless" interface. As a result of massive software-writing efforts, there are some services that now afford users with even the most minimal exposure to computers access to online databases.

The services detailed in this chapter are simple to use for novice or moderate computer users because they are "menu driven." There is no connection to food here. A menu, in computerese, is a kind of index that gives you several choices (or entrees) in the database. It is an alternative to the more extensive search language that most databases require for routine searches. Although they are more time-consuming, menus guide users to databases and specific information easily by giving multiple choices. A menu page to an online service might look like this:

1. Marketing/Sales Information
2. Financial Data
3. Product Information
4. Return to Previous Menu
5. Help

When you choose one of the above, it will lead you to another menu, which lists the offerings under the main menu selection you chose. Eventually, this system is designed to get you to the information you need, which will be in the form of an abstract (summary), full-text article, list, or numeric data. The systems described in this chapter all use this information retrieval method. It is the easiest to learn: you can pick it up the first time out.

On this type of system, you are generally charged for the information you select plus the connect time you use in finding it. Most systems also allow you to bill directly to your credit card.

Although menu-driven services are boiled down and simplified, more experienced users might consider them as a springboard to the more complex services found in the following chapter.

TELEBASE SYSTEMS

As one of the first producers of a user-friendly interface, Telebase—and its founder, Richard Kollin—are at the forefront of this technology, presently making hundreds of databases available to the first-time, inexperienced, or casual computer user. Telebase engineers have written master software that will dial and search more than 700 databases. Users simply dial into the Telebase system, provide billing information, and are presented with a series of menus that ask them what kind of information they are seeking. They are also given the opportunity to search a database by name, if they happen to be familiar with it. The successful search will lead to an abstracted article (or hundreds of them). The system will then list the results of the search. From there, you can pay for what you need.

Telebase provides its services to a host of information vendors as well as through its own direct enterprise—EasyNet. Each service is essentially the same. You can access the Telebase-licensed services through Western Union's EasyLink in a subservice called InfoMaster or through Compuserve's I-Quest. Yet another Telebase service is tailored to librarians' needs. The least expensive way of using Telebase is directly through EasyNet. Compuserve and EasyLink have additional membership and connect charges. However, if you are already a member (or are becoming one) of Compuserve or EasyLink, it might be more convenient for you to search through those services.

Costs

How much does this friendly service cost? It varies, depending on how much information you retrieve, based on flat rates. EasyNet, for example, charges twenty cents per minute connect time just to use the system. Infomaster charges fifteen cents a minute and charges you nothing when you find an item (Compuserve does charge per item). Compuserve's I-Quest charges from ten cents to fifty cents per minute and seven dollars per search. On EasyNet, once you choose a topic, you are charged eight dollars for the search. If you choose to see abstracts, they are two dollars apiece. There is a ten-dollar charge for photocopying, a five-dollar handling charge, and twenty dollars for express delivery.

All the additional charges are similar on all Telebase services. If you don't know what you're looking for, you could be in for an expensive session, so have your search outlined as best you can before you dial in. There is also a bevy of additional charges.

Using the Systems

The main benefit of Telebase systems is that you can access them quickly and around the clock. EasyNet can be dialed directly by calling (with your computer) 1-800-327-9638 or through a local network number. Contact Western Union or Compuserve to obtain information on their Telebase counterparts (see next chapter). Telebase gives you the ability to search bibliographic, numeric, and full-text databases without having to learn the search language of each database vendor. Online search assistance (where you can talk to an expert searcher) is also available. Additionally, you need no special software to start searching.

Your first choice on a Telebase service is whether to search a specific database or let the system search for you. Only semi- or extremely experienced searchers should take the first option. If you don't know what a database contains, you could be wasting your money finding out.

In order to streamline your search as effectively as possible, you should write down the companies, subjects, or areas you want to research before you log on. When you are on the system, you are being charged for every second. You could waste a lot of money fumbling around for the right search topic. While EasyNet and I-Quest are more for general needs, InfoMaster is tailored a bit more to the business user. Each service, however, will give a choice of becoming as specialized a searcher as you like by presenting the following menus:

PRESS TO SELECT
1. Subject
2. Person
3. Place
4. Organization
H Help (for questions)

and a subsequent menu will offer:

1. Newspapers and Newswires
2. Business, Economics
3. Science, Technology, Medicine
4. Law, Trademarks, Patents
5. Social Sciences, Education
6. Art, Literature, and Entertainment
7. Religion, Philosophy
H Help (in case you have questions)

From here, you can narrow down your search even more, as more menus appear to offer you more options until you get an abstract or full-text article. Your costs are displayed on the screen during and after your search.

One of the most useful services for businesses can be found on InfoMaster. A "Company Name Scan" on that system will be able to tell you anything from financial information to new product introduction on thousands of private and public companies. Some other examples of research applications are:

Company profiles Financial data, SEC filings, news items, brand names, products, patents, officers, plant and branch locations, analysts' reports.

Marketing information Market studies, demographics, advertising, industry overviews, technology updates, strategies, overall competitive intelligence.

Legislative and regulatory changes Updates on tax and business laws, Congressional actions, agency rulings, legislative monitors.

Research and development Access to trade journals, newsletters, market research, newspapers, general periodicals, academic journals.

In summary, each menu-drive interface can search nearly every major business, scientific, or general periodical database. Those databases can be found in Dialog, ADP Network, BRS, NewsNet, Pergamon ORBIT Infoline, VU/Text, and many others.

DIALOG'S BUSINESS CONNECTION

Like Telebase Systems, Dialog found that one of the most efficient ways of reaching more information consumers was to design a menu-driven service that would open up its more popular business databases to inexperienced users.

Most of Dialog—a system that is a collection of more than 250 individual databases—is accessible only if you have extensive training in the rather complicated Dialog search language. This language enables users to find a great deal of information, but it requires months to master and was once known only by librarians and information brokers. With Business Connection, though, Dialog is marketing a comprehensive service for relatively inexperienced computer users.

Using the System

Business Connection is a button-down version of some of the most frequently used Dialog databases. Its menus guide you into areas such as:

Corporate intelligence Analysts' reports, recent developments (news), financial reports, and corporate descriptions and locations.

Financial screening Company balance sheets, income statements, stock price data, financials, and industry comparisons.

Products and markets Analysts' reports, product designs and processes, market shares, lists of manufacturers of specific products, unit costs, and other market information.

Sales prospecting Geographic location, industry type, company size, and company branch location of prospective customers.

Travel planning Dun & Bradstreet's Official Airline Guide schedules and flight and hotel booking service.

The strength of Business Connection is in the company information it provides. It allows you to search databases like Investext (analysts' reports), Moody's, Dun & Bradstreet's private company files, D&B's Electronic Yellow Pages, Standard and Poor's investment information, and the Thomas Registers' product information. Sales-prospecting and product data also are easy to retrieve. As with other menu-driven systems, a series of menus leads you to the information.

Costs

The pricing is based on extensive, not occasional, use. For $120, an introductory package buys you special software, a password to the system, and credit for up to $100 of online time. Beyond that, the rate is $84 an hour plus additional charges for telecommunications, prints, and mailing labels (for any mailing lists you wish to generate). Dialog claims that a typical company report costs from $5 to $50. There are no minimum-usage requirements.

For more information, contact dialog at 3460 Hillview Ave., Palo Alto, CA 94304 or telephone (415) 858-3742 or (1-800) 3-DIALOG.

SEARCHLINK

The newest of the "friendly" services, Searchlink, is sponsored by the National Federation of Abstracting and Information Services and provided by the International Data Group, publisher of *Infoworld*.

Using the System

Like the other services, Searchlink requires no special software, passwords, or expertise. By calling (800) 843-7337 with your modem, you can gain access to major database vendors like Dialog, BRS, NewsNet, ORBIT, and VU/Text. The system also takes your credit card number for billing.

Costs

Unlike the other systems, this service streamlines the pricing a bit. You pay $7.99 per search, $2 per abstract, and twenty-five cents per connect time.

EVALUATING THE FRIENDLY SERVICES

In many ways, the menu-driven services are opening up a new world to millions of computer users. They are welcome additions to the online world. However, if you've been searching on your own for more than a few months, you might find it more cost-efficient to use an information broker or search other services using more powerful language.

As you become more experienced with databases, you will learn what information is stored in which database and you can save some time by looking for yourself. Since I am an experienced searcher, I find it frustrating to go through what seems to be an endless stream of menus to get the information I want. And having the system choose databases for me has proven much less fruitful than choosing databases for myself.

If your search needs are extensive and require a fluent knowledge of database searching, then the friendly services might not be worthwhile for you. You could be better off going to an information broker. If your needs are fairly straightforward—say you only need company financial information—then the friendly services might save you time and money. Your decision hinges on (1) the depth of information you need, (2) the time you have to acquire this information, and (3) your familiarity with computers and databases.

For beginners, the friendly services are comprehensive and easy on the nerves. More accomplished searchers might look elsewhere for better results.

4
SOFTIES: ONLINE UTILITIES

- EASYLINK
- MCI MAIL
- THE SOURCE
- COMPUSERVE
- DELPHI
- BRS/BRKTHRU
- DIACOM
- DOW JONES NEWS RETRIEVAL
- NEWSNET

Whether or not you use a computer to search for information, you should be aware of the following services because they contain a generous "deli tray" of general, business, professional, and special interest information resources.

The following are some recommended *utilities* that are designed for the more experienced computer user. For general information needs, they are good to start with and are listed in order of ease of use, versatility, and costliness. Even if you go to an outside specialist for the information, you should know where information can be found. That way, you can direct your information specialist to a particular service. It could save you time and money.

The utilities are also excellent modes of communication that serve as alternatives to the traditional routes. The utilities' *electronic mail* capabilities (see Chapter Nine) permit text to be sent between two or more computers and form the core of many of these services.

When surveying the utilities, pay special attention to their information offerings. Some of them provide easy access to databases that are marketed through other vendors at premium rates. Some examples: Compuserve's demographic data, The Source's Management Contents version, and MCI Mail's Dow Jones News Retrieval gateway.

EASYLINK

Vendor

> The Western Union Telegraph Co.
> One Lake St.
> Upper Saddle River, NJ 07458
> Telephone: (800) 527-5184; (800) 442-4803 in Texas

Costs

Annual subscription fee of $25 or $25 monthly minimum-usage plan. There is a $25/month charge for a telex number. Volume discounts of ten percent are offered in excess of $1,000. A discount of forty percent applies to all Telex or mailbox traffic transmitted between midnight and 7:00 a.m. EST. The FYI News Service is $.65/minute for 110/300 baud and $.90/minute for 1,200-baud transmission. There are extra connect charges for WATS users and mailbox retrieval. Separate charges also apply to InfoMaster information service (see Chapter Three).

Features

EasyLink compares favorably in the communications arena to any other service. It provides a choice of system messages, electronic mail to other EasyLink subscribers, Telex I and II, Worldwide Telex, Mailgram, Telegram, Cablegram, multiple-addressing messages, computer letters, E-COM (U.S. Postal Service), batch input messages up to two million characters, attention line, priority delivery, notification of delivery, and domestic and worldwide directory service. The FYI news service also has reasonably comprehensive general interest and financial news, although there are better, cheaper services if you are looking for news.

The commands are simple and well explained in the manual, which is free with a subscription. Once, when I sent a telex to a company in England on a Saturday, the system not only told me that I did something wrong the first time and the cable didn't get there, but told me so when I logged on and asked for my mail. The telex did make it the second time, and I got a swift reply. At $2.62, the cable saved me some money over a phone call.

Western Union's Telex transmission system is rather antiquated because it takes the messages you send at 300 or 1,200 baud and retransmits them at 50 baud, which is considerably less efficient. But considering that sending a Telex through your personal computer saves you the $.12-a-minute service charge that you would pay to have another service do it, the savings could become significant. The most promising options are the Telegrams,

Cablegrams, and computer letters, which are your computer-typed messages taken off the system, printed out, and put in the U.S. Mail. Western Union has also contracted with DHL Worldwide Express for two-hour document delivery.

Although the FYI service covers a lot of ground, it is, however, costly because you cannot access it via a local network. You dial into it separately from EasyLink on a WATS (800) number. There is an additional charge of $.20/minute to use the WATS line, which Western Union passes on to you, the customer. An EasyLink customer representative told me that WATS line charges are $.70/minute, as opposed to $.50/minute with a local network. I was on FYI no more than ten minutes and it cost me around $16. You get better news service rates elsewhere.

MCI MAIL

Vendor

MCI Communications
2000 M Street, N.W.
Washington, D.C. 20036
Telephone: (800) MCI-2255; (202) 293-4255

Costs

The basic start-up cost is an $18 *Mailbox* fee. Instant Mail is $.45 for up to 500 characters in length; 501 to 7,500 characters in length are $1 with $1 more for each additional 7,500 characters. The Paper Mail ranges from $2 (U.S.) or $5.50 (International) for an MCI letter up to three pages to $8 (U.S.) and $12–$30 (International) for an overnight letter, and $30 for a four-hour letter, which can only be delivered in the U.S. Telexes are $.25/minute through the MCI system and $.43/minute to another carrier.

The service also gives incremental volume discounts

for bulk mailings. There is an extra charge of $.15/minute for WATS access. Graphics can be sent by special arrangement at $20 per graphic. Mail Alert is $1 per message. Dow Jones News Retrieval is billed at DJ's standard rates. Volume-based billing options are available.

Features

MCI is a really basic service that courts all notions of corporate expediency. Although not sporting as many features as EasyLink, MCI Mail's forte is the Instant Mail service, which is an instantaneous service that can be typed on your personal computer and sent through MCI. The service also has access to the Telex network and a gateway to Dow Jones News Retrieval, which is a good companion to have.

In addition to the graphics delivery service, MCI will also print MCI letters on your own letterhead, provided that you register that letterhead with them in advance. Volume mailing is also available. If you want to use the system to store your mail messages, you can do so at $10 per month. All the letters are printed on a laser printer, so there is little likelihood of problems with print quality.

Although $2 to send a letter might seem high, if there is a sense of urgency behind the message, that is an entirely acceptable cost. Naturally, the cost escalates depending upon the speed at which you need a message delivered. MCI's service appears to be a good one for the most time-sensitive correspondence. The graphics-sending feature will pay for itself in no time.

THE SOURCE

Vendor

Source Telecomputing Corp.
1616 Anderson Rd.

McLean, VA 22102
Telephone: (800) 336-3366; (703) 734-7500

Costs

A one-time registration fee of $49.95 includes registration, ID and password assignment, and The Source manual. There is a monthly minimum of $10/month, which applies toward usage. Connect time charges range from $21.60/hour Monday through Friday from 7:00 a.m. to 6:00 p.m. and $7.75/hour from 6:00 p.m. to 7:00 a.m. A surcharge of $5/hour applies to 1,200 baud use during the day and $3/hour extra during the nighttime hours. Connect time charges from Alaska and Hawaii are slightly higher than standard rates. There are additional charges for value-added services such as Mailgrams ($5.15 each for the first 100 words and $5 each for 101 mailgrams or more and 201–300 words) and E-COM ($1.35 each, limit of two pages). Sourcemail, rate schedule, suggestion box, and member information are included in the basic package. Other value-added services range from $44.75/hour during the day and $34.75/hour during the nighttime hours. Rates for special interest groups range from $.18/minute to $.10/minute.

Features

The most appealing aspect of The Source to any business person is its connection to a growing online community through its bulletin board system. There are general bulletin boards and business bulletin boards. Sometimes the bulletin boards are little more than classified advertising for goods or services, but, at other times, they are messages focused on special interests. Through Sourcemail, you can communicate to as many of these bulletin boards as you want and at a relatively low cost. Sales leads may abound here.

The Source used to be known as the "hobbyist's computer tool." No longer. It used to have a membership of mostly computer enthusiasts and amateur programmers who signed up on The Source's myriad of specialty bulletin boards. While those people are still a part of The Source's following, the service has become more attractive to business in recent years. The Source offers a number of communications functions at a relatively low cost. It will even set up a private network for a company or organization.

For research needs, there is Information on Demand, which will do document retrieval and research. Although the research is done by estimate, the document retrieval is competitively priced. For $14 an item or $9 for a government document, IOD will find conference papers, technical reports, census data, patents, 10Ks, specifications, competitor's brochures, or magazine articles. When dealing with IOD, it helps to know exactly what you need. Having IOD do *all* the research for you could be very costly.

Another research-oriented tool is a limited version of Management Contents, the bibliographic retrieval service owned by Ziff-Davis. Management Contents on The Source has only a small number of periodicals from MC's full database. It is good for general business research, but little else. Its search capability is also limited.

The Source also has a general and business news service that does an adequate job in providing hourly updates and the latest financial quotations, but pales in comparison with Dow Jones on the business side.

It's hard to say whether many businesses actually transact deals on the bulletin boards, although they have tremendous potential for such a purpose. The Source's conferencing option seems to have the most potential for corporate communications. Keep in mind that Sourcemail only gets you in touch with Source members, who may or may not be potential business contacts.

The most useful value-added service The Source offers is Investext, which profiles companies on the basis of reports from major brokerage houses. The unique quality of Investext is that it will include some carefully detailed insights into the future earnings potential or products of a particular company while providing the basic facts. Investext is also available on other services. On The Source, Investext is perhaps the single most expensive option. But, if you need the kind of scrutiny a brokerage house can provide in sizing up the competition, Investext could be well worth it. Members can also publish their own newsletters on the system for an additional fee, an option that could have some promotional value for your business.

COMPUSERVE

Vendor

Compuserve, Inc.
P.O. Box 20212
5000 Arlington Center Blvd.
Columbus, OH 43220
Telephone: (800) 848-8199; (614) 457-0802

Costs

After you pay a $35 application fee, there is no minimum for the Consumer information service. The Executive service, however, has a $10/month minimum-use fee and is available for $10/month extra on the Consumer service. Connect rates range from $12.50/hour to $6/hour for day and nighttime hours respectively on 300 baud and $15/hour to $12.50/hour for 1,200 baud. In addition to the Compuserve connect charges, there are also local area network telecommunications charges that range from $.25/hour at night to $14 /hour during the day. All stock quotes, airline schedules (OAG), investment information, and premium Executive services are extra. Business accounts are available. Compuserve also sells its own communications software. Users guide is $14.95.

Features

The Consumer service features I-Quest, news, financial wires, stock quotes, and electronic mail. The most useful business application could be the Disclosure II database on 9,500 public companies. The reports provide basic financial data on the firms and the names of more than 150,000 corporate officers.

The Business and Executive services tout an enhanced electronic mail network, conferencing, professional forums, online travel services, airline schedules, and an executive news service from the Associated Press. Stock quotes, Standard and Poor's company profiles, and Disclosure II SEC reports are on the Executive service. The news on Compuserve provides a full platter derived from several different sources. As part of the Consumer service, you get AP, Business Information Wire (Canadian Press), *USA Today*'s Update and Decisionline services, and Stevens Business Reports. The Executive service provides the *Washington Post*, Money Market Financial Services, Evans Economics Electronic News Service, Agri-Commodities, News-a-Tron Market Reports, the FOI: Newsline (FDA information), and the Canadian Press.

While the Business service is designed for heavy corporate time-sharing needs, the Executive service can be accessed from the Consumer service (same log-on) for an additional $10 a month.

Of the communications options, a device called CB Simulator, an online conferencing service, is very popular. Compuserve also has its own electronic mail system by which it is possible to save money on internal corporate communications, link a whole sales/marketing team nationwide, and have all the features of Compuserve to boot.

Communicating on the Executive service involves using a system called InfoPlex, which can be set up within a company to link branch offices. A separate service called

Interchange can allow a company to communicate within itself and use its own database. For small businessmen and -women, Compuserve makes a special effort to reach out with its U.S. Entrepreneur's Network, an electronic extension of the Entrepreneur's Institute. The service is both a bulletin board and resource library.

One extremely useful attribute of the Executive service is Supersite, a gateway that allows access to demographic information on nearly any area in the country. Supersite, which uses census information, is instrumental in new product planning, sales territory mapping, ACORN reports on neighborhood profiles, and sales potential information.

I was much more impressed with the capabilities of the Executive service than those of the Consumer service. If there is one frustrating factor about the Consumer service, it is that there are a lot of menus to plod through to get what you want, unless, of course, you know the page number. Once you know the name or number of the page you want, it's simple. But you'll probably want to read through the hundreds of different databases. It took me about eight hours to do so. That's a search in itself, since there is so much information on Compuserve. Either service can get extremely expensive quickly if you spend too much time exploring layers of menus and not actually using the service.

The Executive service provides a wide array of investment research in Value Line, Standard and Poor's, Institutional Broker's Estimate Survey, and Disclosure II. If you are researching a public company, chances are that one or all of these services will be of great help. You can find one company profile in less than one minute. If you compare that to the few hours that it would take to send one person to the local library, you may discover that the investment services could save you some money and time.

Of all the general videotex services, Compuserve has the most accessible and fairly priced service for business.

And, with its constantly enhanced command structure, it continues to get easier to use. It's not perfect, but it can be a convenient economic information tool.

DELPHI

Vendor

General Videotex Corp.
3 Blackstone St.
Cambridge, MA 02139
Telephone: (800) 544-4005; (617) 491-3393

Costs

There is a $44.95 "lifetime" membership fee that will be charged after one free day of use if you choose to subscribe. Connect charges range from $.16/minute during the day (7:00 a.m. to 6:00 p.m. weekdays) and $.11/minute during "home" time (6:00 p.m. to 7:00 a.m.). Canadian connect time is $3/hour more. Unless you pay by credit card, you will be assessed a $3.50/month billing fee. News and other premium services start at $20/hour. The handbook is $21.95.

Features

Of the so-called "utilities," Delphi has the best approach to attract businesses and home users.

The most useful feature is Delphi's gateway to Dialog, the information retrieval service. Delphi is the only one of the "general" services that offers the gateway, which, in turn, allows you to access more than 200 business and professional databases. Although Delphi's short primer on how to search Dialog is no substitute for Dialog's own training, it's a good way to see the type of information that's available on Dialog. In addition to Delphi's online charges, you also pay Dialog's rates for online usage, which range from $45/hour to $150/hour. For investors, Delphi has an online brokerage service, stock quotes, and market reports.

The special interest groups are areas on the service that cater to either professional needs or particular subjects. For instance, the writer's network offered typesetting, mail, and research services. The typesetting costs $2/1,000 words.

Combined with UPI News, banking, online publishing and shopping, games, bulletin boards, E-COM, and an encyclopedia, Delphi has assembled a worthy line-up of information providers and services. For those who need the service to help them organize their lives, Delphi has an online scheduler that will keep an appointment calendar and diary. One human touch worth mentioning is Delphi's Oracle (that's what they call it), an online advice service. An additional service that works with Delphi is Grouplink, a private network that Delphi will set up "for as little as $5,000." This system has the ability to access Telex, electronic mail, other databases, classifieds, and conferences.

I don't recommend accessing Dialog through Delphi without a good, working knowledge of Dialog. Nevertheless, it is a worthwhile gateway to have. Because you can avoid having to log on to two different systems, you get a "one-stop" shopping effect. Delphi comes highly recommended, not as a communicator, but as a business tool that can operate on several fronts at once.

BRS/BRKTHRU

Vendor

BRS Information Technologies
1200 Rt. 7
Latham, NY 12110
Telephone: (800) 345-4BRS; (518) 783-1161

Costs

One-time subscription fee of $75. No monthly minimums. Connect charges range from $17.50/hour to $82.50/hour depending upon which of the sixty-five databases you are using. Standard rates apply during the day, and reduced rates go into effect at night and on the weekends. Document charges are extra and vary for each database.

Features

Unlike the utilities, BRS/BRKTHRU is best used as a business research tool because it mainly offers online databases. Sister services BRS/Search and BRS/After Dark offer similar databases that require knowledge of search languages.

BRKTHRU is a menu-driven service that gives you a search language with which to pry as much information as possible out of the databases. The two main business information databases are represented by Management Contents and ABI/INFORM. Industry Data Sources will give a researcher even further insight into specific industry groups and markets.

For sales and marketing specialists, there are Predicasts' Annual Reports, PROMT, and F & S Index. These databases will have anything from entire annual reports to new product introductions. The Index of Frost and Sullivan Market Research Reports rounds out the collection with a time-saving guide to market research reports that can be ordered.

Although the rest of the service should mostly appeal to academics, educators, engineers, and medical researchers, BRS has assembled one of the most comprehensive services at reasonable rates—especially if you use it at night. The only drawback is that you will need to be fairly comfortable with database searching to reap the most useful information from the system.

For the money, the selection of databases on BRK-

THRU makes it a natural for business research needs. The PTS files are especially useful in tracking down specific product or market research items. And the combination of Management Contents and ABI/INFORM make the service a comprehensive and pragmatic choice for intermediate online database users.

DIALCOM

Vendor

Dialcom, Inc.
1109 Spring St., Suite 410
Silver Spring, MD 20910
Telephone: (301) 881-9020

Costs

You or your company must sign up for a contract minimum in one of three different plans from $100 to $2,500 per month, depending upon how much the service will be used. Contract terms are either monthly or yearly. There is a two-tiered online-time pricing system ranging from $10.50/hour for the one-year contract for prime-time usage to as low as $6.50/hour for non–prime-time usage. Prime time is Monday through Friday from 8:00 a.m. to 5:59 p.m. EST. Non-prime is Saturday, Sunday, and all national holidays and from 6:00 p.m. to 7:59 a.m. Monday through Friday.

Electronic mail is $1 per message for the first 1,000 characters and $.50 for each additional 1,000 characters. Dialcom has a link to the Telex and Telegram systems, which are billed at standard international carrier rates. Extra charges exist for ABI/INFORM ($28.50/hour), electronic publishing ($4–$6/hour), file transfer, database management, news services ($15/hour), electronic clipping service ($1 per term per day), Official Airline Guide, and gateways to other databases. Except for free OAG and local network guides, most documentation costs from $3 to $30.

Features

For lack of a better term, Dialcom is an integrated communications manager. You can conduct a conference online and put your own calendar schedule on the system for your personal perusal. It's possible to create your own database of documents or publish your own material, store it or have it printed out. The system even has an online text and spelling editor. The only thing Dialcom has forgotten is to send your mother flowers on Mother's Day.

An especially useful feature is the news-clipping service, which will scan the newswires (AP, UPI, OPEC, Deutsche Presse Agentur, International Medical Tribune, and the U.S. Department of Agriculture) if you enter a particular subject. Any related stories will be waiting for you when you log on. You can also check current airline schedules on OAG.

Obviously, you'd have to use the service quite a bit to justify its cost. If your communications needs are small or if you are a casual user of the news or ABI/INFORM services, Dialcom is not suitable for you. However, if you have a whole department that needs to have the synergy of constantly updated information; online conferencing; and gateways to OAG, Dow Jones, and the news services, Dialcom could be the right package.

DOW JONES NEWS RETRIEVAL

Vendor

Dow Jones, Inc.
P. O. Box 300
Princeton, NJ 08543
Telephone: (800) 257-5114; (609) 452-1511 in New Jersey

Costs

Standard membership is $49.95 per password and a $12 annual service fee after the first year. Blue Chip membership gives you one-third off on non–prime-time usage and a $95 yearly subscription. Executive membership gives you one-third off on prime and non–prime-time usage and requires a $50/month subscription fee. With the Blue Chip and Executive plans, you get six hours of time free on selected databases. Basic services such as Dow Jones Business and Economic News cost from $1.20 to $.80/minute during prime time, 6:00 a.m. to 6:01 p.m. EST), and $.20 to $.13/minute during non–prime time. Dow Jones quotes range from $.90/minute during prime hours and $.15/minute for non–prime time for the standard service. The rates for quotes on Blue Chip and Executive service are slightly less. Free text, financial and investment services, general news, and MCI Mail are all at higher hourly rates than the basic service, ranging from $1.20/minute to $.40/minute.

Features

Dow Jones is nothing less than the dean of business database vendors. As far as market intelligence, corporate news, or Fortune 1,000 coverage goes, DJNR is a prime source of information. It is also one of the most expensive online utilities on the market. Dow Jones offers everything from in-depth economic analyses to the hourly Dow Jones news wire updates, but the business of Dow Jones is undeniably investment-related information.

On the news side, there is Dow Jones News Service, the *Wall Street Journal,* and *Barron's.* The DJ service carries the breaking business stories that other services might pick up hours later. If you don't have the time to read the full text of the stories, there is the Wall Street Journal Highlights Online, which contains summaries of major stories from the *WSJ.* This section includes headlines, front page, back page, market pages, and editorial columns.

SOFTIES: ONLINE UTILITIES 63

If you need background on a news event or a profile of news about a particular company, it's possible to search a file of Dow Jones News that goes back to 1979 and a *Wall Street Journal* file that covers the past year. Of all the Dow Jones services for news retrieval, this is the most refined. It's possible to track week-by-week news on major companies this way. For additional, more specialized company information, DJNR also has Standard and Poor's profiles of 4,600 companies that include earnings and dividend and earnings estimates. Profiles on public companies are also found in Disclosure II's SEC file, Media General's Financial Services and the Forbes Directory.

On the investment side, DJNR's platter of quote services covers stocks, commodities, options, money markets, foreign exchanges, Dow Jones averages, and bonds on a delayed or real-time basis. The system will even update up to five profiles of twenty-five companies each.

DJNR subscriptions include MCI Mail. Other supplementary services include general news, sports, weather, an online encyclopedia, Comp-u-store online shopping, *Wall Street Week* transcripts, Official Airline Guide, Peterson's College Selection Service, and a Medical and Drug Reference guide.

The most essential part of the service is the free-text search capability. Although it has its own set of commands, it's a powerful feature that will search by year, industry code, and root words or locate "hot" business news. Any much-needed current research on a public company could start here.

One criticism of DJNR that is echoed by information brokers is that it covers major public companies and the markets extremely well but is slack on the smaller, private firms that are not in the Fortune or Forbes 500. For that type of information, turn to Dun & Bradstreet's many services.

For the money you'd pay for Dow Jones, you'd have to have the service for daily information needs. Use of the free-text search alone will cost $1.20/minute. That's $72 an hour! There are less-expensive business research services. But if you need to know something as it happens, it's difficult to scoop Dow Jones. Dow Jones customer representatives suggest that, if your DJNR monthly bills are more than $25/month, the better value would be the Blue Chip membership.

NEWSNET

Vendor

NewsNet, Inc.
945 Haverford Rd.
Bryn Mawr, PA 19010
Telephone: (800) 345-1301; (215) 527-8030

Costs

The monthly subscription fee is $15. Pricing for prime connect time (8:00 a.m. to 8:00 p.m. EST) is $24/hour at 300 baud and $48/hour for 1,200 baud. For non-prime access, it's $18/hour (8:00 p.m. to 8:00 a.m. EST). There is a 200 percent premium over the 300-baud rate for 2,400-baud access. Unless you are already a print subscriber to the newsletters in the service, you will pay a premium rate of $24/hour to read eighty percent of the newsletters. Other premium services such as VU/Quote (stock quotes) and TRW credit reports are $36/hour. Some newsletters cost as much as $120/hour to read.

Features

NewsNet specializes in industry newsletters, general business news, and credit reports.

It's important to take a good look at what NewsNet offers before you get a subscription. NewsNet is a very good informer that will do many things for you automatically. But, like any other service, you have to know what you need.

A genuine timesaver on NewsNet that might make it pay for itself is the NewsFlash function. You can select up to five subject keywords that the system will search for you automatically from selected newsletters, the PR News Service, a corporation information wire, or the UPI News. This feature will track any new developments in a particular industry, company, or subject category. If you don't have time to scan hundreds of publications and the news wires, NewsFlash is an efficient electronic clipping service.

Another electronic clipping service is *USA Today's* Decisionline, which will give you daily updates in Trends, Issues, Travel, Technology, Banking, Legal, Insurance, Energy, and urgent bulletins. *USA Today* also has a news service called Update that is more general in nature.

The most powerful and unique value-added service on NewsNet is the TRW Company Profile section. At $29 per report (plus connect time), TRW will give you credit data, payment background, financial information, and business facts on more than two million public and private companies. This is a condensed version of the credit-reporting service for which TRW was charging several thousand dollars a year for a subscription. This is an invaluable service that is not (at this writing) available on any other system.

In addition to the Official Airline Guide and Investext, NewsNet gives you an online version of the *Sales Prospector,* a newsletter that gives you sales leads by geographic area. The Prospector is detailed at greater length in the sales/marketing section of this book. Other useful services include BNA's Online reports on taxes, congressional actions, and summarized reports for executives; the International Business Clearinghouse bartering service; Reuter's news reports; and the Jiji Press Ticker service from Japan (translated, of course).

NewsNet is essential for any infocentric manager who needs the most current information on competition, markets, sales leads, or newsletters. It is not as well rounded as the other services, but for specialists who need NewsNet's credit, business research, and newsletter information, it's a valuable resource.

5
THE CORE OF
THE ELECTRONIC
PROFIT CENTER

- DUN & BRADSTREET SERVICES
- D&B: AN OVERVIEW OF APPLICATIONS
- D&B DATABASES: A SPECIAL ABILITY
- ADDITIONAL D&B MARKETING SERVICES
- ELECTRONIC YELLOW PAGES
- INSTANT YELLOW PAGES

Steven Arnold, (then) vice-president of Data Courier, Inc., observed in a corporate intelligence seminar that there is a "move to recognize that the flood of business information matters must be marshalled and disciplined." Why must business information be "marshalled and disciplined?" Because there is so much of it, and so much of it means very little to you. It's hard to find what is important, especially when you just don't have the time.

In building your electronic profit center, the first concept to remember is that information is like an unmanageable river that flows all the time. At certain times, it spills over its banks to invade your territory, unless you have a way of controlling it. By controlling it, you channel it into your electronic profit center.

Discipline is important in controlling the costs of mounting a market research, competitive intelligence, or sales/marketing campaign. Since Dun & Bradstreet (D&B) estimates that the average sales call costs a company more than $200, becoming infocentric also means saving money.

D&B and other services in this chapter help you do this by screening prospects, organizing your sales force, and defining your competition's strengths and weaknesses. This helps you pare down the ten to twenty percent of sales calls that industry analysts claim are wasted in the average campaign. The services also give you a comprehensive range of valuable information. The following services offer the most fundamental infocentric benefits.

DUN & BRADSTREET SERVICES

D&B has progressed from *just* a credit-reporting service to a full-service information company in the last few years. With their information and organization, they can conduct a complete telemarketing campaign or analyze and refine your marketing strategy.

THE CORE OF THE ELECTRONIC PROFIT CENTER 69

The D&B family comes very close to being a complete supermarket for business information. Not only do they produce, collect, and store their own information, they market, distribute, and deliver it any way you like it.

Many of the most commonly used D&B databases are found in Dialog or through Dialog's Business Connection service. The best way for the novice or moderately experienced user to access D&B databases is through Business Connection, EasyNet, InfoMaster, or I-Quest. Only highly trained users should try to search D&B databases through Dialog. As with all the databases listed in this book, you also have the option of using an information broker or librarian for your search.

The following is a profile of current D&B services. The prices on each service vary, depending on what you need. This is but a small sampling of what D&B can do.

Costs/Information

Since D&B provides such a broad range of services, the cost of the service depends upon the application. All the D&B databases are available on Dialog. They range in price from $60 to $135/hour plus additional charges from $.05 to $74 per record requested. D&B, although a real buffet of business information, services its databases through different units operating under the same roof. That means Dun's marketing, credit, travel, and demographic databases are all handled by different divisions. For more information, contact your local D&B office or call (201) 299-0181; (201) 455-0900; or (800) 223-1026. The following is an overview of D&B services.

Credit services All the information that D&B acquires through its various services comes from several databases. All told, the company collects numbers on more than five million U.S. and Canadian companies. Their most familiar database is probably the credit information one. Until recently, only subscribers on annual contract had access to the credit information. Now, that data can be obtained instantaneously via personal computer or by telephone via D&B's DunsPrint services. For information, call (201) 464-7803 or (800) 526-4590. These services can be used for market intelligence, competitive intelligence, and credit reporting.

DunsDial, for current D&B subscribers, will give a company's general background and detailed credit history over the phone and follow it up with hard copy within one to ten days, depending upon what priority you assign to it. DunsPrint is a computer service that offers credit services through your personal computer or terminal. A more comprehensive screening service called DunsQuest will allow you to sort credit data by company size, net worth, sales, and other factors. DunsVoice will produce a computer-directed voice to read a company's latest D&B rating and follow up with a complete report by mail. For more information, call (800) 526-4590. In New Jersey, call (201) 464-7803.

D&B's Market Identifiers (DMI) Originates from the same DMI file as the Million Dollar Directory (below). DMI primarily includes business establishments with ten or more employees or with $1 million or more in sales. The information is updated quarterly and includes business locations, branches, corporate linkages, number of employees, sales volume, percent change in sales, square footage of facility, sales territory, banks and accounting firms, chief executive officer, and SMSA code and name. This is *the* file on private firms. DMI can be used for competitive and market intelligence, mailing lists, telemarketing, and corporate profiles.

The Million Dollar Directory Provides a breakdown that applies to businesses with net worth of $500,000 or more. The database is also smaller, with 120,000 businesses, versus 1. 4 million in DMI. Both databases are in Dialog or in print version.

Dun's Financial Records Contains the same data as Market Identifiers, only in spreadsheet format listing assets and liabilities. Offered jointly by Dun's Credit and Marketing units.

International Dun's Market Identifiers This is a compilation of 500,000 businesses located in 133 countries outside of the U.S. It isn't as extensive as DMI, but includes CEO, SIC, gross annual sales, international trade indicator, control, parent company background, number of employees, and subsidiary denotation. DMI, MDD, and IDMI are on Dialog. For more information on business reference services, call (800) 526-0651 or (201) 299-8228.

Moody's Investors Services Several databases oriented more toward investment information than basic business information. Company overviews and profiles are available on 3,800 public companies listed on the NYSE and AMEX stock exchanges and 1,500 actively traded OTC companies.

Moody's Corporate Profiles Contains business descriptions; interim earnings and dividends; quarterly developments; analyses; five-year records on earnings, balance sheets, book value, P/E ratio, and price range; and capitalization and SIC codes.

Moody's U.S. Corporate News Tracks developments of about 18,000 companies. These are the same reports found in the time-honored Moody's manuals. The file is updated weekly and focuses on earnings, mergers and acquisitions, management changes, stock offerings, bond ratings, balance sheets, and annual reports. An excellent source on current public corporate news.

Moody's International Corporate News Covers more than 5,000 companies. The topics are similar to those covered in the U.S. version. For more information on all Moody's services, call (800) 342-5647 or (212) 553-0857 in New York, Alaska, and Hawaii.

Donnelly Demographics and Marketing Information Services D&B did what a lot of other companies have done and culled a bonanza of information from the U.S. Census Bureau. Supplemented with and augmented by its own data and related services, Donnelly offers extensive information on given populations within defined geographic areas. You can get information from as large an area as the whole country or as small as a square block. Donnelly can detail basic population information, educational backgrounds, housing, mobility, occupation and industries, employment status, family profiles, persons per household, marital status, and breakdowns by age, sex, and race. It is used most often for market intelligence, site and market planning, sales targeting, and new branch site locations.

This service links market information with geographic areas. Donnelly can break out the numbers with any possible combinations. The file is so extensive that it takes eight pages to describe what's in it. Also included is psychographic information in the Clusterplus package. American Profile provides lifestyle information on target groups. Although some of Donnelly's information is available on Dialog, it's difficult to search. Donnelly's support staff is separate from the Dun's Marketing group, so staff members are specialists in demographics. This is but a small sample of what Donnelly provides. For more information, call (800) 527-DMIS or (203) 965-5400. The main office is located at 1351 Washington Blvd., Stamford, CT, 06902.

Thomas Cook Travel USA A corporate travel agency that will book airline tickets and hotels, monitor corporate travel expenses, provide a twenty-four-hour, toll-free "hotline," and discount corporate rates. For more information, call (800) 237-5558.

Official Airline Guide (electronic edition) D&B's most visible service, because most of the utilities listed in the previous chapter offer a "gateway" (premium rate access) to OAG. The service allows you to read airline and hotel rate schedules and book through your personal computer. It's available twenty-four hours a day.

D&B: AN OVERVIEW OF APPLICATIONS

Information by itself is but a lever. In order to make your electronic profit center work smoothly, you need a variety of fulcrums—especially when using D&B services.

Here are a few essential facts about D&B. First, nearly every database is accompanied by a full complement of services. The services allow you to use the information to your best advantage in an endless stream of applications. Of course, if you're able to retrieve the information by yourself, that is the cheapest way. D&B will do simple things like generate mailing lists or design whole marketing strategies. You need to know what you want first and establish a hierarchy of needs. Of course, the more you want, the more it costs.

The following list summarizes the categories in which D&B excels:

General business information Provides extensive addresses, telephone numbers, company/branch locations, executives, number of employees, sales volume, line of business by SIC or DUNS numbers, parent company, branch locations, geographic information by zip and telephone area code, and three-year sales trend data.

Sales prospecting Through several services, D&B can identify future clients. By giving your salespeople complete company information before they make cold calls, you can ensure that the first contacts will be far more productive.

You can also create a sales lead list from a database of companies that are similar to current customers.

New product analysis One of the best ways to determine a new product's position is by examining what the competition has on the market. Several databases detail new product information within company reports.

Territory analysis It's possible to divide territories on the basis of potential for particular products. This process goes hand-in-hand with market analysis. Map out new areas for expansion. Also redefine old ones.

Customized marketing programs D&B can integrate market research, sales prospecting, new product analysis, and territory analysis. D&B, a full-service marketing company, has the resources to give you a few company profiles or mount a telemarketing campaign.

Credit reports Originally the core of D&B's business, now more accessible to personal computer users.

Demographics Donnelly Demographic's services can give you detailed information on specific geographic areas.

D&B DATABASES: A SPECIAL ABILITY

D&B has the unique ability to track any company in its databases through one number that it assigns to each company. To no one's surprise, this is called a DUNS number. Unlike the U.S. government, which assigns largely outdated SIC codes to describe businesses by industry group, the DUNS numbers can find a company more efficiently. If you know a DUNS number, the D&B databases can be searched in a second. If you don't, D&B can find what you're looking for by numerous other methods.

ADDITIONAL D&B MARKETING SERVICES

Sales Prospecting Service Like many list house/brokers, D&B will generate tailored lists from its previously described databases. The lists are available in hard copy or on magnetic tape. Tape is generally more expensive. For under 10,000 names, the price could be as high as $635/thousand (M). Get up to 50,000 names, and the price drops to $230/M. The information is available on prospecting cards or on mailing labels. Besides addresses, telephone numbers, and contacts, the service provides sales volumes, employees at location, parent company, corporate affiliations, industry indicators, SMSA names, and branch or franchise information.

Market Analysis Profile D&B will look at your business activity and map out key markets.

Customer Analysis Service D&B will define your customers and generate a list of names that match the characteristics of your "best" group.

Market Segmentation Service A more comprehensive program that identifies top prospects while defining market strengths.

SalesNet A broad telemarketing program. D&B will generate a list of prospects, write the scripts, provide the callers, and capture the results.

Financial Profiles D&B does some number crunching by pulling numbers from its databases for analysis and sales prospecting. The service will take a firm's financial data and present it in a spreadsheet format, comparing it to same-size companies in the same geographic area. The service has numerous applications for sales/marketing, credit management, merger and acquisition monitoring, bank management, strategic planning, and corporate planning. As part of the service, D&B has done industry studies, accumulated average financial data on more than 800 lines of business, and designed an online system to analyze the information. This is where infocentrics reaches its peak. Some of the data can be inserted into a Lotus 1-2-3 program. For more information, call (201) 665-5330.

Direct Response Services In conjunction with its other services, D&B will sell you lists for direct marketing. Dun's Decision Makers file has the names, addresses, and other pertinent information on more than 8.5 million executives. They also have a file titled Executive Women.

Sales Force Management Service D&B will meet with your sales/marketing people and propose how to plan, cut costs, save time, and increase revenues. Depending on how much service you need, D&B can measure market potential, establish sales quotas, redefine territories, and evaluate results. This is the premium service that D&B Marketing offers to corporate clients.

A. C. Nielsen Yes, D&B even owns the television rating company that does extremely comprehensive market research. Nielsen's specialty is consumer market research and analysis. It's a bells-and-whistles company by itself that will measure anything you want. Test marketing and retail sampling also are Nielsen's strong suits. For more information, call (312) 498-6300.

ELECTRONIC YELLOW PAGES

D&B's Electronic Yellow Pages (EYP) is a recently acquired online database service that has information on ten million U.S. businesses. Many of the businesses, typical of Yellow Page listings, are "Ma-and-Pa" operations,the small firms that really are at the backbone of the U.S. economy. There are also the big businesses, their branch offices, and many private professional firms that might be difficult to track down.

The EYP is "a compilation of all 4,800 yellow-page phone directories, plus data from more than 1,000 sources, stored online and accessible by industry, or by company's name." That's Market Data Retrieval's definition. I choose to think of EYP as a sales/marketing instrument that is constantly getting better.

Some of the applications for EYP include:

Pure sales lead generation Done by SIC, city, company name, and/or branch location, state, population code, telephone area code, and zip code.

Territory definition and alignment EYP will tell you how many businesses of a certain type or SIC code are in a given area. You can redeploy your sales force accordingly.

Market/competitive analysis Lists retailers, service firms, financial service institutions, wholesalers, construction-related firms, and manufacturers and describes their businesses, net worth, number of employees, and parent companies. Answers the basic question of who's already there in the marketplace.

Site planning Since its strength is the ability to search by city, state, telephone area code, or zip, you can determine how many businesses will be near your new retail or service location.

Marketing Generates lists for test marketing, telemarketing, and research purposes.

EYP is accessible through Dialog, Dialog's Business Connection, EasyNet, InfoMaster, and I-Quest. It will serve your purposes well to be informed about the service. Since it is entirely electronic, it is "searched" rather than read in a library. All the information retrieved from a search can be printed offline by Dialog and sent to you in less than four working days. If you need the information immediately, and you don't mind paying up to $60 an hour for the connect charges, then you can have a list in a day, provided you don't want more than about 100 names. The average search should run about ten to twenty minutes. An even easier way of getting a list is through the sales-prospecting function of Dialog's Business Connection.

If you have a personal computer in the office and choose not to go through a broker or librarian, you may need to know the SIC codes of the companies or group of companies you are targeting. That can be a disadvantage. You'll also need to take the special training class that Dialog offers in EYP. EYP can be downloaded with the proper software. EYP has also provided offline printing on mailing labels at an extra charge.

Particularly useful features of EYP enable you to track or identify companies in a specified telephone area code, city, state, branch location, or zip code. That's extremely valuable when generating leads in a finite geographic area. List brokers may not be able to find new prospects in these ways.

EYP is also instrumental in locating businesses for purposes of competitive monitoring, market research, and demographics.

Costs

You pay anywhere from $.05 (for the index search) to $.20 per full company record and $60 an hour in connect charges. Mailing lists are $.10 per record.

If you need several thousand leads, however, you might be better off going to a list broker. Despite the fact that EYP has no minimum list orders, about 1,000 names on EYP will cost more than $250. EYP's specialty is pinpointing small businesses within a certain area, not generating names and addresses in bulk.

Using the Service

To use EYP, you must understand how it is set up in Dialog. First, it is not just one service, but several. It should be noted that, if you are searching EYP through Dialog's Business Connection, you won't need to know the following information as the Business Connection software will choose the subservices for you. If you are searching directly through Dialog, however, you need to know how to use:

The Index The place to start if you don't know which EYP file to search. It will locate the proper file. You can start your search with as little as one SIC code.

Financial Services Directory Covers banks, savings and loans, and credit unions in the U.S. This file includes not only headquarters locations but branch offices as well. Subject searches can cover banks (unspecified), commercial banks, savings banks, savings and loans (unspecified), S & Ls (member S & L Ins. Corp.), S & Ls (member FSLIC), credit unions (unspecified), federal credit unions, and state credit unions. You also can locate an institution by asset size, city, state, telephone area code, zip code, and population code.

Professionals Directory Covers professionals in real estate, medicine, insurance, law, engineering, accounting, hospitals, medical laboratories, and clinics. All told, sixty categories of professionals are searchable by SIC. Professionals can also be found by advertising class (in the actual yellow pages), county name, city, company names, office size, population code, and number of beds (hospitals). This can be a hard group to find reliable data on when generating leads. Because most of the information comes from telephone directories, you can be sure that it's updated at least twice a year.

Wholesalers Directory There are more than 180 SIC categories that can be searched. As with the other directories, the companies may be located by telephone area code, zip-code, city, state, advertising class, company name, and population code. This is a good way to find distributors, suppliers, service centers, and specialty goods wholesalers.

Retailers Directory One of the largest EYP files (three files on Dialog), offering a choice of more than 200 SIC categories to search. The range of retailers covered includes general merchandise, food stores, clothing, furniture, automobile dealerships, restaurants, building supplies, and service stations. One notably important feature is the ability to search by trade name. For example, say you want to find the addresses of K-Mart stores within a certain zip code. It's possible with EYP. This file is a key resource for site planners who need to scout the competition within a geographic area.

Construction Directory Lists a wide range of contractors engaged in new building, additions, repairs, earth moving, plumbing, painting, and electrical work. More than seventy-five SICs are searchable. This is a good method of locating the "little guy" trades that you may not be able to reach through any other company directories or lists.

Services Directory A catch-all, generic file that covers all the businesses not listed in previous files. Some of the services include motels, cleaners, advertising agencies, direct mail, employment agencies, data processing, equipment rental, movie theatres, sports clubs, and detective agencies. What you won't find in the other files might be in this one.

Manufacturers Directory Although it probably does not contain enough detailed information, this file has listings on each establishment. In addition to the standard EYP search features, you can locate companies by net worth and number of employees. Industries covered include food products, lumber, chemicals, primary metals, petroleum, machinery, transportation equipment, and miscellaneous products.

EYP Drawbacks

Despite the obvious utility of EYP, there are some drawbacks. The most prominent one is that it relies upon the four-digit SIC system for indexing. The four-digit SICs, as most reference librarians have reminded me, is out of date and due to be updated in the next five years by the government. Until then, there is a problem of searching for companies you have targeted that may not have SICs describing their line of business. High-technology companies get short shrift in this area.

Another shortfall, where other D&B services are strong, is the lack of contact information on executives or other people whom you need to talk directly to in closing a deal.

The cost of the information is based upon its exclusivity. It is relatively current, unlike many lists, which might contain mailing addresses from outdated magazine subscription lists. Additionally, EYP is remarkably powerful in generating names of businesses with just a few employees. Most business databases focus on large corporations.

Once you understand how to search EYP, getting information from it is the most efficient process imaginable. It qualifies as an infocentric manager's extension of the electronic profit center. For more information, call (203) 926-4800, (201) 299-0181 (in New Jersey), or (800) 223-1026. Customer inquiries can be addressed to Dun's Marketing Services, 49 Old Bloomfield Ave., Mt. Lakes Corporate Center II, Mt. Lakes, NJ, 07046.

INSTANT YELLOW PAGES

The Instant Yellow Pages (IYP), owned and operated by American Business Lists, Inc., has created a service that is very similar to EYP—except that it is available in a number of different ways. Unlike EYP, it is not on a huge system like Dialog. IYP markets its fourteen million business listings directly to the end-user.

The source for the IYP is the same as for its rival. IYP has stored and indexed the information from 4,800 U.S. Yellow Page directories. It has more of a list-house marketing philosophy and claims to ship lists within twenty-four hours of receiving the order. You don't have to go through a broker or librarian to get the lists, either.

IYP can be searched by SIC number, zip code, brand/speciality/franchise, and keyword. Like EYP, IYP would allow you to locate all the veterinarians in Dogpatch, if you wanted to (it would help if you knew the zip code, though).

If you simply want lists from IYP, they are available in many forms including mailing labels, prospect lists, 3$_{oo}$ 5$_{oo}$ cards, magnetic tape (ASCII or EBCDIC languages), IBM-PC compatible diskettes, 8$_{oo}$ IBM-3740 diskettes, and online retrieval.

Costs/Information

A fairly standard pricing structure makes IYP potentially more economical than EYP. Based on a minimum order of $75, IYP's pricing ranges from $.015 per name (mailing labels) to $.08 per name (on magnetic tape or diskette). IYP accepts company checks, American Express, MasterCard, or VISA.

The online service, accessible by most terminals or personal computers, carries a minimum annual subscription of $95 ($60 per year renewal rate), $.10 per record, and $1 per minute connect time. There also are telecommunications charges, which could be substantial, considering that you would have to access IYP on a long-distance line, unless you live in or around Omaha. You would save money by letting EYP do the work.

One major disadvantage is that IYP provides much less flexibility than EYP. It is a much more limited service than EYP except in the states of Iowa, Kansas, Minnesota, Missouri, Nebraska, North Dakota, and South Dakota, for which IYP has full yellow-page listings.

Where IYP surpasses EYP, however, is in economy of scale. It is more cost-effective to obtain a list of several thousand names from IYP than from EYP. IYP also ships lists promptly and has a customer service department.

Although not directly related to IYP's service, American Business Lists will also broker you a list that it can't generate from IYP, provide market research, and can obtain lists of farms and Canadian businesses.

For more information, you can call IYP at (402) 331-7169. It is located at 5707 South 86th Circle, P.O. Box 27347, Omaha, NE, 68127.

6
SPECIALIZED DATABASES FOR COMPANY ANALYSIS

- INVESTEXT: COMPANY AND INVESTMENT INFORMATION
- TRW CREDIT REPORTS
- SEC REPORTS ONLINE
- SALES-PROSPECTING DATABASES
- THE SALES PROSPECTOR
- TRADE AND INDUSTRY ASAP
- THOMAS REGISTER ONLINE FOR INDUSTRIAL MARKETING
- TRINET: DETAILED COMPANY INFORMATION
- SITENET
- VU/TEXT: NEWSPAPERS ONLINE
- DATA TIMES

INVESTEXT: COMPANY AND INVESTMENT INFORMATION

In doing research, you'll find a great deal of information on public companies. Many sources, like SEC reports and PR Newswire, are really companies reporting on themselves. They therefore give a biased view of their companies' condition. These reports usually contain reliable glimpses of a company's financial health, but they are not critical enough because they don't have an independent perspective.

Investext, an electronic service of the Business Research Corporation, casts critical eyes on 7,500 public corporations. Analysts from more than forty top brokerage and investment banking firms scrutinize every phase of a company's operations in Investext. The main strength of Investext is that the research is being done by industry experts and contained in reports that are usually released only to customers of the investment firms.

The analysts' reports in Investext cover a wide universe of information not found in SEC filings or annual reports. It is possible to search Investext by company name, product, industry, or subject. The most immediate uses for Investext are:

Market analysis The service details market share forecasts, growth rates, supply-and-demand ratios, sales forecasts, consumer spending habits, and production figures.

Financial and competitive analysis The reports contain profit-and-loss statements, quarterly and annual results, cash flow models, product cost and margin analysis, capital expenditures, debt structure, and a balance sheet.

Business planning Because the reports also focus on industry overviews, you can extrapolate trends for an entire industry. Featured in the reports are divisional forecasts, lines of business reporting, five-year sales and income models, production/shipment estimates, earnings forecasts, and analyses of sales and operating income by business segments.

Corporate profiles Investext gives you a clear-cut picture of a company's past, present, and future. Emphasizing marketing strategies, new products, management changes, and growth projections, the service excels at complete background sketches.

The most powerful way of retrieving information from Investext is through Dialog. On Dialog, it's possible to search Investext by analyst, company name, company symbol, corporate source, industry group, SIC, and ticker symbol. Investext is also available directly from the vendor in a service called Investext/Plus.

NewsNet and The Source also offer Investext, but there are limitations on the ways in which you can search their databases. NewsNet, for example, has its database broken up into twenty-two different industry groups. Since some of the companies overlap in several industry groups, it can be difficult to find exactly what you want. NewsNet has keyword searching, which can be less versatile in locating specific items.

As far as corporate intelligence goes, Investext has the inside track on mainstream corporations. The only drawback to Investext is that it covers publicly traded companies exclusively. But for what it does cover, Investext has no peer.

Costs/Information

The costs of Investext vary greatly, depending on which system/vendor you use. On Dialog, for example, Investext costs $96/hour plus $4.50 per record. On NewsNet, you could pay up to $120/hour. For more information on Investext, call (800) 662-7878 or (617) 350-4044 or write to the Business Research Corp., 12 Farnsworth St., Boston, MA, 02210.

TRW CREDIT REPORTS

Like Dun & Bradstreet, TRW does a tidy business in reporting individual and company credit conditions to other companies. If you are a TRW subscriber, you pay a hefty annual subscription to receive the reports—that is, if you meet TRW's stringent requirements. Until recently, that was the only way of getting TRW reports.

If you are a subscriber to NewsNet, you can gain access to TRW's Business Profiles database. Although TRW doesn't give a complete financial picture of a company, the credit information is invaluable and hard to find. Searching on TRW is relatively simple even if you misspell or don't know the exact name of a company, because the system will give you at least two companies that resemble what you selected.

In TRW's NewsNet service, about 400,000 companies are covered. All told, about eight million business locations are included. To make the profiles more complete, Standard and Poor's has added business and financial data.

TRW profiles provide an excellent way of determining the financial health of a company through its bill-paying records. More importantly, the reports offer vital information on cash flow and key liabilities. The profiles are insightful in the shrewdest possible ways. The reports also contain:

Key facts Basic information includes sales figures, number of employees, the year the firm was established, and names of chief officers.

Trade payments TRW will break out payment trends from records of the accounts receivables records of their suppliers. Quarterly and seasonal payment patterns, five-quarter trade payment totals, and a comparison with the payment patterns of other companies in the same line of business are contained in the Trade Line Industry section of the report.

Financial data Standard and Poor's provides a balance sheet, operating statement, critical ratios, an In-Depth Business Background, and a Summary Background.

Public information For certain states, TRW provides additional information on federal, state, and county tax liens; bankruptcies, judgments, satisfactions; Uniform Commercial Code filings; and bulk transfers. This section gives a unique look at a company's legal liabilities.

At this writing, not all the TRW profiles were accompanied by Standard and Poor's reports, although NewsNet assured me that it was in a continuous process of updating them. Despite inconsistencies here and there, the service promises to become an affordable and efficient tool that will make basic company profiles extremely accessible.

Costs/Information

The initial price per report is $29 plus NewsNet connect charges ($36 an hour at 300 baud). In addition, you'll need a NewsNet subscription. For more information, call NewsNet at (800) 345-1301.

SEC REPORTS ONLINE

One steady and relatively inexpensive way of getting a close look at a company's financial condition has always been Securities and Exchange Commission (SEC) reports. However, tracking SEC reports by sending a messenger to an SEC office to pick up a paper report can be costly and time consuming. That's why several services have emerged to tap SEC's extensive database, thus circumventing the hard-copy chase.

The SEC requires that companies with at least $3 million in assets and at least 500 shareholders of one class of stock must file forms stating general and specific information about their lines of business and financial conditions.

One key source for SEC filings, other than the SEC's regional and Washington offices, has been Disclosure, which is available in several forms. Disclosure II and Disclosure's "Financials" databases, cover 30,000 companies. They are available on Dialog, Compuserve, and Dow Jones News Retrieval. In addition to financial data and general corporate backgrounds, Disclosure II is good at tracking:

Acquisition or tender offers Public companies must file notices of these occurrences.

Material events or corporate changes SEC filings are a prime place to discover stock ownership changes, earnings estimates, changes in management, disposition of assets, or other important financial events.

Legal proceedings SEC reports will give updates on litigation against or initiated by public companies.

Exhibits, contracts, or other material agreements Any major event that will affect a company's financial statements must be reported to the SEC.

Financial statements A complete accounting of the company's business(es) is provided.

Management information Executive changes are reported.

As part of a subscription service called Watch, Disclosure will automatically send you specific reports on selected companies. A separate, less selective subscription service is also available.

The online database, Disclosure II, is also available on magnetic tape and through a personal computer service called MicroDisclosure. The principal advantage of the online services is their ability to search by company, subject, line of business, and several other descriptions.

MicroDisclosure is essentially a software package tailored for IBM personal computers that allows you to talk to the database in relatively simple language. The package costs $45, and you pay additional connect charges of $.75 per minute and $3.50 for each financial statement you store.

Disclosure also markets demographic information that is based on U.S. Census Bureau statistics.

Costs/Information

The costs of Disclosure vary, depending upon the vendor. Dialog, for example, charges $45/hour plus $11 per record. BRS, Mead Data Central, and VU/Text also carry Disclosure databases.

For more information on the online services, contact the individual vendors or call (800) 638-8076. You can write Disclosure at 5161 River Rd., Bethesda, MD, 20816.

SALES-PROSPECTING DATABASES

In the information age, simply buying names and numbers from mailing list houses may not be enough. Sales prospecting has become more sophisticated.

The experts in the business of generating sales leads have networks of information at their disposal that could be accessed by you. Sales lead generation is often a matter of reading the business sections or newspapers for press releases of new construction, plant expansions, or business relocations. You have to be a good reporter to get the scoop on sales leads. The infocentric way, however, works much more smoothly.

THE SALES PROSPECTOR

One of the experts in sales lead generation is Prospector Research Services, Inc., in Boston. The company publishes the *Sales Prospector,* a monthly report on sales leads by fifteen U.S. geographic regions. Although the print report is available for $125 a year per region or $895 a year for the entire country, it's the electronic version that's an infocentric instrument.

The *Sales Prospector* gleans sales leads from construction projects, industrial and commercial expansions, and relocations. This type of item might be buried in a local newspaper section and more than likely will never make the *Wall Street Journal*. The leads are important because they imply a future need for goods and services. The *Prospector* even follows through to name executives involved in the project and architectural and engineering firms expected to be doing the work.

While focusing mainly on leads for the building trades, the *Prospector* is also a source of leads for office suppliers, industrial equipment manufacturers and distributors, and wholesalers and jobbers of all types.

According to Thomas Ireland, vice-president of marketing for Prospector Research Services, it takes as little as fifteen seconds to customize a report on NewsNet and less than two minutes to go through three regional reports. In addition to geographic designations, the leads are coded by sixty-nine industry groups and can be searched by keywords in NewsNet. Keywords are like little flags that go up when a computer searches a database. It makes company names, locations, and other searchable items immediately accessible.

The most infocentric quality of the electronic *Sales Prospector* is that one searcher can find in a few minutes what a whole sales staff might take a week to ferret out. There are no reams of copies to read, no delays while phone calls are being returned. You get what you search for on the Prospector by picking the area or industry group you want.

The NewsNet version also allows for downloading into personal computers, printing, and searching by date of report. NewsNet also lists the Sales Prospector under three of its own industry classifications—general business, real estate, and construction. NewsNet also has a feature that will allow you to search the Prospector by SIC code.

Costs/Information

Accessed through NewsNet, the Sales Prospector allows you to search the entire report on a pay-per-view basis. Subscribers, of course, qualify for a discounted rate. All told, you pay $60 an hour plus telecommunications charges to read Sales Prospector on NewsNet, which you must subscribe to first if you want the Prospector. *Sales Prospector* (print) subscribers pay only $24/hour. Nonsubscribers pay $60/hour.

Because the Sales Prospector retrieves only the reports needed, it is an efficient sales lead management device. For more information, call NewsNet at (800) 345-1301 or Prospector Research at (617) 899-1271.

TRADE AND INDUSTRY ASAP

Trade and Industry ASAP is similar to the Sales Prospector in that it tracks business developments on a local or regional level. Formerly called Area Business Databank, it is actually a part of Information Access Company's Trade and Industry Index database, an index of twenty local and regional U.S. and Canadian business publications. Topics, company names, and geographic locations can be checked in the index. The primary uses of the database are:

Local business climate analysis Because a great deal of this information is not available on any other service, it's a key method of determining business activity on a local or regional level.

Sales prospecting Pick up on local developments and construction projects that could mean an opportunity to bid on supplies or services.

Labor climate analysis Local publications are more likely to cover local labor disputes or settlements. General labor market profiles are included.

Competitive analysis See what companies are doing in specific locations; e.g., plant expansions, shutdowns, or relocations.

Business and site planning Determine the business climate for a given area by scanning publications from the region.

Costs/Information

Pricing depends upon the system on which you are using this service (Dialog, BRS, etc.). The Dialog version costs $84/hour plus $3.50 per record. For more information, call (800) 3-DIALOG.

THOMAS REGISTERS ONLINE FOR INDUSTRIAL MARKETING

Thomas Publishing Co. produces the big, green books that most industrial marketers refer to when they want to find out who makes a certain product. The Thomas Registers have been cataloging manufactured products for seventy-five years and they don't seem to be waning in popularity. But Thomas has gone one step further. It went online with Dialog.

Although you can find the Thomas Registers sitting comfortably in most libraries, the online service promises to be an infocentric necessity for industrial marketers.

Why is the online version so important? Because it gets you to large volumes of information without wasting several hours of valuable time. In the hands of a trained searcher, it can yield results quickly and cheaply. The online service covers 123,000 U.S. companies that supply 50,000 classes of products.

Thomas is famous for its ability to track products by trade name, identify manufacturers, and give important background material on both. The database can be searched by company name, city, state, area code, trade name, and zip code. If you don't know the exact name of a product, the system will give you many approximate names from which to choose. That's a crucial advantage over the print version.

Searching the online service also allows some flexibility in finding product manufacturers. Terms can be linked so that the system will search for metal—fabricators and fabricators—metal. An exact listing is not necessary. The same principle applies to trade names. Other search options will allow you to track companies by telex number—an option I haven't seen on any other database.

Some applications for Thomas Online include:

Competitive and product analysis Identifies a broad range of products made by U.S. companies. Products are listed by standard and trade names.

Sales prospecting Allows you to build lists by finding companies in a particular line of business that are likely to buy your product or service. Management contacts and telex numbers are contained in the company profiles, so calls may be made directly from the search printout. Also useful for telemarketing.

Market research and planning Details available on size of company, number of employees, current addresses, product lines, and corporate affiliations. Thomas will tell you the resources the major players have at their disposal.

Costs/Information

The only real disadvantage of Thomas Online is its price, which at $100/hour and $1.50/record, is one of the more expensive online services. But for the quality of the information on trade-name products, it could be worth it to match products with companies in a competitive or market analysis. The whole process could take seconds instead of weeks—instant market research. A companion database, Thomas New Industrial Products, is a bargain at $95/hour. You also could access the Registers through Dialog's Business Connection. For more information, call (212) 695-0500 or (212) 290-7291.

TRINET: DETAILED COMPANY INFORMATION

Trinet has two files on Dialog—the Company and Establishment databases. These databases contain basic information on all companies with twenty employees or more, including address, SIC, employment, sales, and parent company name.

Searches can be performed to locate companies by primary SIC, two-digit primary SIC, and three-digit primary SIC. A salient feature for marketers is the fact that market share is given for each company. The difference between the files is that the Establishment file focuses on single or branch locations of a company while the Company database covers multi-establishment companies.

The company database also gives a breakdown on nonmanufacturing sales, manufacturing sales, total sales, number of establishments, and non-U.S. sales. These are important figures for competitive analyses. Some recommended uses for Trinet are:

Market and competitive analysis Because Trinet gives you sales and market share figures together, it's easy to get a complete picture of a specific market, especially when you can also search the databases for companies in one SIC group.

Sales prospecting The company profiles give marketers an insight into lines of business. Lists of companies can be generated by geographic area, telephone area code, or SIC.

Trinet is one of the few database producers that offer direct marketing support services. The company will provide market research, telemarketing, and consulting on marketing problems. Line-of-business reports that analyze company market shares and lines of business also are available in print form.

Costs/Information

Searching Trinet on Dialog costs $90 an hour for both databases. There is an additional charge of $1.60 per record for the Company database and $.50 per record for the Establishment database. For more information, call (212) 267-3600 or (800) 3-DIALOG.

SITENET

Costs/Information

At last, something for free. Well, almost. Sitenet, a service of Conway Data, Inc., won't charge you anything for accessing its database on area business surveys. All you pay is local telecommunications charges because it's available through the Uninet network.

Sitenet is unique because it is a wholly advertiser-supported service that makes its money from some of the businesses that list on the system. Geared toward industrial real estate development, the service has online information on industrial parks, office space, and residential developments.

Sitenet has what it calls "hotlists" of available office buildings, office space, and office/industrial park sites. The database can be searched by country, state, and city. (Some Canadian information is provided.) A notably pragmatic section called Contacts lists local planners and industrial real estate agents by city. This is a good resource guide for local development project information.

There is some demographic information, but that

hardly seems to be Sitenet's strength. The database is much better at industrial real estate matters. Some specific uses for Sitenet are:

Location analysis Because it details industrial real estate activity in certain geographic areas, Sitenet can give important leads on local business activity.

Sales prospecting New developments mean an implied need for goods and services. Industrial parks are sales territories in themselves.

Site planning Sitenet contains good background for executives considering relocations.

Although Sitenet is far from complete in its coverage on a national basis, it can cover major metropolitan areas fairly well. It's a growing service. For the price, it's one of the best bargains around. For more information, call (800) 554-5686 or (404) 458-6026.

VU/TEXT: NEWSPAPERS ONLINE

This Knight-Ridder service contains the text of thirty major U.S. newspapers and business information from more than 2,000 business publications. It is a broadly based, newspaper research service that replaces what journalists call a "morgue," which is the room where all the old back issues are kept.

Publications on VU/Text are generally full text with the exception of Predicasts' PROMT database, which contains article abstracts. Other services on VU/Text include Associated Press wire stories, PR Newswire, ABI/INFORM, VU/Quote (stock quotations), *Wall Street Week* transcripts, *Academic American Encyclopedia,* and Disclosure.

Newspapers represented on VU/Text span the gamut from the *Washington Post* to the *Sacramento Bee.* Since Knight-Ridder owns a few newspapers, its publications are also in the database. Time, Inc., magazines such as *Time, Money, Fortune,* and *Sports Illustrated* are also found on VU/Text. The service also supplies databases from the *Financial Times,* the *Economist, Asahi* (Japan's largest daily paper) News Service, TASS (Soviet news service), and the BBC *Summary of World Broadcasts.*

If you have a specific reason to search one of VU/Text's periodicals, you can call VU/Text directly. The majority of these newspapers are not found on any other vendor's service.

Costs/Information

Hourly prices range from $75/hour to $295/hour, depending upon the database. For more information, call VU/Text at (800) 258-8080 or (215) 665-3300 or write to 1211 Chestnut St., Philadelphia, PA, 19107.

DATA TIMES

Like VU/Text, Data Times is a newspaper-oriented service of forty general, business, and financial databases. It is, however, smaller and more specialized. Unlike VU/Text, it can be accessed through Dow Jones News Retrieval.

In addition to the AP Newswire, Data Times provides full-text articles from the *Arkansas Gazette* to the *Seattle Times.* A useful service called LegisTrak, which tracks legislation as it plods its way through Congress or state legislatures, is also available.

Costs/Information

Hourly rates range from $60 to $90, depending on which rate plan you choose. There is a one-time subscription fee of $50. For more information, call (800) 642-2525 or (405) 843-7323. You can write Data Times at 818 N.W. 63rd St., Oklahoma City, OK, 73116.

7
REFINED RESEARCH TOOLS

- INFORMATION ACCESS COMPANY AND DATA COURIER: THE TWIN TOWERS
- IAC SPECIALTIES
- KNOWLEDGE INDEX: A RESEARCH BARGAIN
- PREDICASTS: MARKET RESEARCH ONLINE
- ADTRACK
- MEAD DATA CENTRAL
- DOING THE RESEARCH: SEARCHING TIPS
- DOING THE SEARCH

By far, one of the best applications for online database searching is research. Not only can individuals or businesses save on the costs of subscribing to hundreds of publications, but they can also search subjects by company, industry, product, or any number of descriptors. The general research functions of several key databases anchor the electronic profit center.

INFORMATION ACCESS COMPANY AND DATA COURIER: THE TWIN TOWERS

In addition to Dow Jones, D&B, and PTS, there are two companies that provide important online business databases. These are the Information Access Company (IAC) and Data Courier, Inc. These database vendors aid infocentric companies in consulting, market research, company profiles, industry trend analysis, corporate and competitive analysis, new product announcements, labor relations, and market planning.

IAC owns and operates Management Contents, a key business periodical database that abstracts more than 700 publications published from 1974 to the present. IAC also "publishes" the Trade and Industry Index, which includes the *Wall Street Journal* and PR Newswire; Industry Data Sources, which focuses on marketing, product, and financial information by industry; The Magazine Index, a collection of 435 general interest periodicals; and Newsearch, a daily updated file containing the *New York Times, Wall Street Journal,* 370 popular magazines, 660 law journals, and six law newspapers.

Data Courier produces ABI/INFORM and Business Dateline, versatile business periodical databases containing abstracts from more than 500 management and business journals. While ABI/INFORM taps a broad range of business publications and is available through Dialog and a number of other systems, Business Dateline, a full-text service, specializes in local and regional publications. ABI/INFORM features abstracts on everything from *ABA Banking Journal* to the *Wharton Magazine*. It is available on Dialog, Dialcom, and BRS.

When you search ABI/INFORM, you can either use Data Courier's "controlled vocabulary" of pre-selected business topics, a DUNS number, or the Dialog or BRS search languages. Each of these methods can get very complicated. Know what you want to search before you search or find a competent librarian or information broker.

Business Dateline focuses on popular periodicals like *Crain's Cleveland Business* and the *Mississippi Business Journal*. It has a much more regional business concentration that is useful in spotting industry trends, company expansions, or relocations; executive movement and profiles; and general marketing research. Unlike the widespread availability of ABI/INFORM, Dateline is available only on Dialog, Dow Jones News Retrieval, and VU/Text.

Costs/Information

The cost of these services varies, depending on the system on which it is accessed. Each system has different hourly rates and telecommunications charges. Dialog, for example, charges $81/hour. Data Courier and the other vendors also provide document delivery service, which ranges from $6.75 to $8.25 per article. Data Courier also offers a facsimile delivery service that can send articles to any worldwide location within hours of the order.

You can contact Data Courier, Inc., by calling (800) 626-2823; (800) 626-0307 (Canada); or (502) 582-4111.

IAC SPECIALTIES

All IAC services are available on Dialog and through the other major vendors like Mead Data Central and BRS.

Management Contents is also available on The Source in limited form.

Between the two companies (IAC and Data Courier), it's possible to read nearly any business periodical published in the U.S. The major infocentric advantage is that you read what you want to read. If you can use one of these systems, it's simple to find what you want in a minimum amount of time. IAC, however, offers a broader range of abstracted publications, which are subdivided into these services:

Management Contents Indexes and abstracts more than 700 journals, proceedings, books, courses, newsletters, tabloids, and research reports. Unique features include the ability to search by company name, author, title, corporate source, DUNS number, product name, publication, ticker symbol, or ISBN number. A prime source for any published material on businesses in 300–500 word abstracts.

Trade and Industry Index A file (full text in its ASAP version) that also includes the PR Newswire, a source for corporate press releases; the *Wall Street Journal;* 330 journals; and selected entries from more than 1,200 other publications. Broad subject coverage of major industries is one of the file's many strengths. It also has 720 legal publications indexed. Special features include searching by SIC, publisher, geographic location, journal name, author, and ticker symbol.

Industry Data Sources A more refined resource for the market researcher, this file concentrates on sixty-five major industry groups by abstracting market research reports, investment research, forecasts, directories, yearbooks, newsletters, monographs, dissertations, conference papers, and other databases.

The Magazine Index A file (full text in ASAP version) more suited for tracking popular literature. Covers areas related to current affairs, consumer product evaluations, social science, cultural events, science, technology, and agriculture.

Newsearch Ideal for keeping abreast of recent developments through general circulation periodicals and newspapers. The file combines magazines, newspapers, and law-journals. Will do customized searches on subjects.

IAC also publishes databases that specialize in legal topics and computer hardware and software, and even sells software that will aid you in searching them.

For nearly every research application from an executive profile to industry trends, IAC databases contain a plethora of good, easily accessed information. IAC will also print mailing lists from its *Ward's Business Directory*.

Costs/Information

Again, costs vary depending on the vendor you're using. IAC databases on Dialog, for example, range from $75/hour for Industry Data Sources to $90/hour for Management Contents.

You can contact Information Access Co. at 11 Davis Dr., Belmont, CA, 94002, or call (800) 227-8431; (415) 591-2333.

KNOWLEDGE INDEX: A RESEARCH BARGAIN

Other than getting a subscription to Dialog—something I don't recommend for novice or intermediate computer users—one of the best ways of doing general research is to subscribe to Dialog's Knowledge Index.

Knowledge Index is perhaps the least expensive online library available. It takes some time to learn how to use, but, as a research tool, it has no peer in its class since it offers thirty of Dialog's more popular databases. Their subjects range from education to technology.

Although it is clearly a bargain to most novice or intermediate users, Knowledge Index has one drawback: it is available only on weekends and evenings. That makes it a good "corporate homework tool," but it may be of little use if you need it during business hours. Nevertheless, I've used it quite often at home and find it worth the wait.

For someone who has a moderate amount of computer experience, Knowledge Index is extremely useful. It's not particularly desirable, however, for beginners. Like most online databases, it requires that you learn a simple search language. After a few hours of practice, you can use the service efficiently. It is not as simple as Dialog's Business Connection, but it can give you greater control over the information you retrieve. It is particularly helpful in researching company developments, popular literature, competitive analyses, corporate profiles, executive profiles, general news, competitive intelligence, and new product development. Knowledge Index databases include:

Standard & Poor's News Full-text coverage of more than 10,000 publicly held U.S. companies from June 1979 to the present.

ABI/INFORM, Trade and Industry Index, Magazine Index, Newsearch, National Newspaper Index A well-rounded selection of general and business periodicals.

Knowledge Index also has databases for professionals who choose the "search-at-home" route. For health care professionals, there are Medline, International Pharmaceutical Abstracts, and BIOSIS Previews. Engineers could benefit from Engineering Literature Index and NTIS (National Technical Information Service). For legal professionals, there is the Legal Resource Index. Agriculture, publishing, psychology, computers, and education are some of the other areas of interest.

Familiarity only increases the value of Knowledge Index. There is a short payback period if you use it frequently and find good information.

Costs/Information

The pricing for Knowledge Index is simple—$24 an hour plus telecommunications charges. Once you pay a $35 start-up fee, you get two hours free, which is a generous amount of time on an online system. You can access it through Telenet, Tymnet, Uninet, or Dialnet. Copying charges range from $6.25 to $12.25 for rush orders.

Because Knowledge Index is being marketed to the home user, it's available from 6:00 p.m. to 5:00 a.m. (your local time) from Monday through Thursday; 6:00 p.m. to midnight on Friday; 8:00 a.m. to midnight on Saturday; and 3:00 p.m. to 5:00 a.m. on Sunday. For more information, call (800) 3-DIALOG or (415) 858-3792 or write Dialog at 3460 Hillview Ave., Palo Alto, CA, 94304.

PREDICASTS: MARKET RESEARCH ONLINE

Specializing in market research, Predicasts' files are generally available on Predicasts' terminal system, BRS, or Dialog, and they serve many roles. These databases are primarily used for market planning and analysis, trend analysis, demographic research, new product monitoring, competitive intelligence, and general business research.

A publisher of abstracted and specialized business information, Predicasts is well known for its PROMT, PTS F & S Indexes, Annual Reports, Defense Markets and Technology, U.S. and International Forecasts, and Time Series. More than 1,500 trade magazines, journals, newspapers, and annual reports are covered in Predicasts' services.

The following is a summary of Predicasts' services:

Business and Industry News More than 1,200 trade and business journals are abstracted in this database. Stories in publications ranging from *Business Week* to *Women's Wear Daily* can be found in the database up to forty-eight hours after they are published in their respective print forms, Predicasts claims.

PROMT A database of company and product information, PROMT is updated weekly and covers more than 120,000 companies with abstracts from 1,200 domestic and international journals. This service is the best way to track specific information on product development.

F & S Index An electronic version of the print product (Frost and Sullivan), F & S details companies, products, industries, demographics, and government regulations. More than three million one- and two-line summaries are contained in this file.

Defense Markets and Technology One of the few databases that cover literature on the defense industry. An important resource for defense contractors.

Annual Reports Abstracts More than 50,000 companies are covered.

Forecasts A market researcher's most basic tool, containing more than 700,000 abstracts of forecasts on products, industries, trends, population, housing, and relevant economic activities.

Time Series Information on economic, demographic, financial, and industrial activity. Subjects such as GNP, imports, end-users, population, and capital spending are included in this largely numeric/statistical file.

The real time-saving function of these Predicasts services is that you can search them by product, company, SIC, and geographic area. Predicasts' best information focuses on products, markets, and forecasts. It can provide excellent background and current awareness on not only U.S. but also overseas subjects.

Costs/Information

Pricing on Dialog ranges from $114 an hour to $150 an hour, but you are paying for the relative exclusivity of some of the information. There are additional charges for offline printing. BRS pricing is similar. A document delivery service and a deposit account are also available.

For periodic and specialized market research needs, Predicasts' services are able to locate relevant information in minutes, if not seconds. The alternative to accessing these online products is searching hundreds of journals by hand, which could take days, or paying hundreds or thousands of dollars to commission market research studies. For more information, call Predicasts at (800) 321-6388 or (216) 795-3000 or write to Predicasts, 11001 Cedar Ave., Cleveland, OH, 44106.

ADTRACK

Adtrack is a specialized service, owned by the Kingman Consulting Group, Inc., to track advertisements by companies. All told, the database covers ads placed in nearly 150 U.S. magazines.

Although most of the magazines are consumer oriented, they can provide good samplings of national advertising campaigns. The database lists advertisements of a fourth of a page or more and can be searched by company, journal, brand name, publication date, ad color, and name of photographer, artist, designer, tester, or spokesperson.

Costs/Information

Pricing on Dialog is $95 an hour plus 25 cents per full record printed offline. For more information, call (612) 646-6558 or Dialog at (800) 3-Dialog.

MEAD DATA CENTRAL

Mead produces and markets three services—Nexis, Medis, and Lexis. The third service is tailored for lawyers and contains a wide range of legal research, journals, citations, and case law. Medis is designed for medical researchers. Nexis, however, was designed more for general business research and has a few features not found on any other database service. Because this chapter deals primarily with general research, I will detail Nexis.

Nexis, unlike most of Dialog, is a full-text medium. It can be used for general or specialized research, depending upon which Nexis database you use. When you retrieve information from it, you have a choice of seeing citations, abstracts, or the entire article or document. A good portion of Dialog databases contain only abstracted information.

As a user of Nexis, the first thing that appealed to me was the training. The training is conducted at regional sales offices by experienced Nexis users. The best part is that it's free and you get more than an hour of free time on Nexis to perform searches. Any subsequent training, such as corporate information applications, is also free. It is possible to learn numerous applications for Nexis in about two hours. It's intensive training that makes you aware of a whole universe of information that can be obtained in a few minutes. You will definitely need the training to use the system. Nexis's search language is complicated but will yield a great deal of information to the experienced user.

Nexis offers several service options. You can either rent the Nexis terminal and printer or receive service on most personal computers.

The Nexis terminal has a special keyboard with buttons specifying Nexis functions. The training is done on Nexis terminals, which can be a disadvantage if you are using a personal computer in your own setting. However, the special Nexis keys become function keys on an IBM personal computer (or compatibles), so it's really no problem. The special Nexis software will dial into the MeadNet telecommunications network and the Nexis computers in Dayton, Ohio. I've used Nexis on the special terminals and the IBM personal computer. I prefer the IBM simply because the keys are larger and I have big hands. Both terminals will do essentially the same job.

You can understand Nexis best by using it or watching a search. Before you even consider using it, though, you need to browse through a Nexis catalog of databases to determine if it can be cost effective for your business. The following is a summary what that Nexis can do:

ECLIPSE This is Nexis' electronic clipping service. This premium service will automatically retrieve articles on subjects of your choosing while you are not using the terminal. The articles that the system finds are automatically printed out and mailed to you. The time and cost savings are enormous.

EXCHANGE A storehouse of public company information can be found here. One file, the National Automated Accounting Research System (NAARS), contains accounting and financial data reports on 8,000 listed and over-the-counter companies. Other research reports in EXCHANGE are prepared by professional research analysts at investment banking and brokerage firms such as Merrill Lynch and the New York Society of Security Analysts. This section also holds SEC filings, Zacks Earnings Estimates, and reports on European countries by major European banks. Applications for EXCHANGE include market and competitive analysis, new product monitoring, merger/acquisition analysis, corporate profiles, market planning, site planning, financial analysis, investment, and general business research.

INFOBANK Containing some of the most influential publications in the world, INFOBANK provides abstracts from key journals from 1969 to the present. Produced by the New York Times Company, the service includes the *New York Times* twenty-four hours after it is published, the *Washington Post, American Banker, Business Week, Fortune, Forbes, Harvard Business Review,* the *Wall Street Journal,* the *Economist,* and *U.S. News and World Report.* There are about sixty publications in this section. Two related news services—TODAY and Business News Update—provide news summaries from the *New York Times.* Full-text versions of the *New York Times* from June 1, 1980, to the present are also available.

Advertising and Market Intelligence (AMI) This subsection of INFOBANK (jointly produced with the advertising firm J. Walter Thompson) contains more than 125,000 abstracts from more than sixty publications specializing in marketing and advertising. Key journals like *Advertising Age, AdWeek, Billboard, Direct Marketing, Marketing News, Sales and Marketing Management,* and the *Wall Street Journal* are abstracted. Special emphasis is placed on product coverage, advertising and marketing budgets for Fortune 500 companies, market shares, demographics, and promotions. This is the marketing/advertising person's tool on Nexis. Ad agencies use AMI to track executive and account changes, billings, ad rates, mergers and acquisitions, company news, and potential new clients. Test marketing, market research, consumer behavior, and government regulations are also covered. AMI is best for market and competitive analysis, market planning, strategic planning, territory analysis, sales prospecting, corporate and executive profiles, trend analysis, news, and general research.

The Library Nexis has full-text articles from a generous sampling of business periodicals. This section encompasses major newspapers, business magazines, trade magazines, newsletters, and wire services like the Associated Press,

United International, PR News, Reuters, Business Wire, Jiji and Kyodo (Japan), Xinhua (China), States News Service, and the Associated Press Political Wire. This is the core of the service that gives a representative selection of nearly every major news source in the world.

The Reference Service A bibliographic abstract section that includes references and abstracts, directories, handbooks, databases, almanacs, and other sources. Files are compiled by the Bank Marketing Association, AMI, Industry Data Sources (Information Access Company), National Technical Information Service, *Defense and Foreign Affairs Handbook, Forbes Annual Directory,* and *Federal Research in Progress Directory.* More recent additions include Management Contents, National Newspaper Index, Newsreach, Trade and Industry Index, Magazine Index, the Computer Database, and Legal Resource Index.

Some examples of popular Nexis applications include:

- Determining the advertising and marketing budget of a competitor by using the AMI file.
- Compiling articles that detail an industry trend through the ECLIPSE service.
- Gathering general and financial information on a prospective client before a contact is made.
- Locating all businesses in one industry group in a given geographic area.
- Tracking the development and marketing of a certain product using AMI and ECLIPSE.
- Reading investment bankers' research reports on a company for merger/acquisition analysis.
- Determining the market for a specific product or service by doing background profiles on companies already in a targeted line of business.

Rounding out the Nexis service is a patent search service called LEXPAT, several versions of the *Encyclopaedia*

Brittanica, and numerous files on published government documents. There also is a tax-reporting service called BNA Online (on Lexis) and software devices to allow you to search specific subject groups or the entire Nexis database.

Costs/Information

Nexis pricing, although it can get complicated, is on a two-tier scale for connect time once you pay a $125 monthly subscription fee. Off-peak searching (7:30 p.m. to 7:30 a.m. local time) is thirty percent off the price of prime-time searching during the day. Peak searching costs $3 to $30 per search (depending on the file searched) plus $10/hour telecommunications time and $20/hour connect time. Printing and ECLIPSE usage charges are extra and vary on volume demands. Terminal and printer leasing are also an additional $65 to $150 charge. Offline prints carry a $15 handling charge plus $.02 per printed line.

For more information on Nexis, or to locate a regional sales office, call (800) 227-4908, (513) 865-6800, or write Mead at P.O. Box 1830, Dayton, OH, 45401.

In order to use Nexis cost effectively, you'd need to project weekly information needs. It isn't worth it to pay for Nexis on a casual, less-than-weekly basis. If you use it less than, say, $75 a month, you are not getting your money's worth from Nexis.

Even if you don't need Nexis in the office, most brokers and librarians use it. However, if you choose a middleman (or woman) to do the searching for you, you need to familiarize yourself with Nexis offerings before you order information.

DOING THE RESEARCH: SEARCHING TIPS

Whether you appoint someone to search a database or search it yourself, if you follow a few, simple rules, your search will be done efficiently and at the lowest possible cost. These suggestions were gathered from reference librarians and information brokers from across the country. You should follow these guidelines before you begin your search:

Identification What do you want? Companies? Executive names? Branch locations? Sales volume figures? Figure out what you want before you even make a call. Define your problem and identify your strategy. Can you get it at the library, or will you need a broker?

Locating the information Where is the information you want? Is it contained in one of the databases described in this book? Is it in print or electronic form? Which service could get you the information the fastest? A library? A broker? A list house? Yourself?

Costs Know what you should expect to pay for the information before you go to a broker or online. Get the approximate costs of a search plus delivery and/or printing costs up front from brokers. Will it be more cost effective to do a database search than to use conventional methods? For example, Dialog databases Arthur D. Little, FIND/SVP, and Industry Data Sources might locate a $1,500 market research report and summarize it for you. This could save you money.

Also, prepare a budget and timetable before you search. Most successful searches for one to five (simple) subjects cost under $50 and can be done in a day's time. Detailed market research will cost more.

Definitions Know how you or the searcher will get the information. Will they search by SIC, DUNS number, company name, zip code, or state? If so, it would help to know that information before beginning the search. Specify your terms, try to get exact spelling of companies or persons (a misspelled name will not locate what you want). Use a thesaurus, if necessary, to describe a subject area in several different ways. Many databases use "controlled terms"; that is, they use specific subject headings for indexing purposes. Be as detailed as possible when discussing your information request with your searcher.

Searching Remember that the meter's running when you or the searcher logs on. Offline prints are much cheaper than online ones. Most services will print offline. Be exact. An inexact set of items to search can be a waste of time. Database search languages, although increasingly better equipped to handle more complicated searches, look for specific names, subjects, and categories. Artificial intelligence hasn't arrived on the online database searching front yet. Be as specific as possible when outlining your search. Tell your searcher dates, names of publications, exact company names, or anything else that will put you on the most direct route to your information. Correct name spellings also make a big difference. Be present during the search if someone else does it.

In short, know when you need a search and when you don't. For instance, some Dun & Bradstreet information such as the Million Dollar Directory and some of Moody's Investors Services are in print. It's far cheaper to stroll to the library to read those books in a reference section. Of course, you have a wide range of search options online that you'll never be able to do with printed material.

Searches may or may not turn up the information you need. If what you need can be found in a general business or trade periodical, chances are that an online database search will find it in a matter of minutes. If you are looking for insights into the Mongolian yak market, you'd be better off going to Mongolia. In any case, successful searches depend upon your presearch preparations.

While this is not a manual on searching or search techniques, there are numerous texts that explain database searching in detail. Consult the Bibliography in Appendix A for further reference. The following section explains how a typical search could proceed.

DOING THE SEARCH

Your search begins before you turn on your computer. Make sure that you have outlined your search and written down important details. The rest is fairly routine and goes like this:

1. Set up your computer and modem. Dial into a local area network such as Telenet, Tymnet, Uninet, Dialnet, Compuserve, or MeadNet. You will be asked for a service number of the vendor you want.

   What Service? _____

   Welcome to *****!

2. If and when you respond with the correct service, the vendor system will ask for a log-on and password. As a subscriber, you should be provided with both. Note that systems like Easynet do not require a password. Your password will not be displayed as you type it.

   LOGON: *******
   PASSWORD: *******

3. The system will now either display a menu or ask you which database you wish to search. From here, depending upon the system, you can use electronic mail, search databases, read subscriber news, or exit system. Most menu-driven systems are self-explanatory. You should have a summary of commands and keywords at your side when using those systems.

With more elaborate systems such as Dialog, use manuals as much as possible. Dialog, for example, publishes "Blue Sheets" that tell how to search a particular database. Your pre-search training in this regard is essential. A successful search will get you the information you are seeking. The file might look like this:

DIGITAL TECH CORP:
Third-Quarter Results

	Earnings Per Share			P/E Ratio		Dividend
52-Week Range	1984	1985	1986E	1985	1986E	
126–75	$5.73	6.25	8.35	16.5	12.3	None

4. At this point, you can either *print out* the report, *store it to disk,* or use the system's *document-ordering* service. The first two options will give you the information immediately. The last one will take a few days. If you've found what you want, you can search other databases, using the proper commands and/or menus.

The best way to learn database searching is to watch an experienced searcher such as a broker or librarian. Even if you don't search by yourself, you should ask to be present during a search anyway, because you might be able to add useful information that will make the search flow more smoothly. Reading search manuals and attending training classes that the vendors offer are also helpful preparations.

If you don't have the time or inclination to search databases, that's understandable. Searching takes some time to learn and master. Nevertheless, you still need to know how database searches work. You'll especially need to follow the guidelines at the beginning of this chapter. If all goes well, you'll walk away from a successful search having saved some time and money. That's the most satisfying part of this infocentric sojourn.

8
GOVERNMENT AND TRADE SERVICES/ DATABASES

- THE TOP OF THE WORLD
- COMMERCE BUSINESS DAILY
- PINPOINT
- THE INTERNATIONAL BUSINESS CLEARINGHOUSE AND THE WORLD OF BARTERING/TRADE

Working with the government needn't provoke fears of tiresome bureaucracies, inefficient agencies, and $700 toilet seats. The government can indeed be a friend to businesses by providing useful databases and services.

The government's most useful business databases are maintained by the Commerce Department and its International Trade Administration (ITA), one of the lowest-profile agencies to emerge from Washington. The ITA is largely responsible for promoting trade by American businesses outside the U.S.

The ITA provides a full range of services to companies currently exporting or planning to enter the import/export business. ITA trade specialists generally act in a consultancy position and access all the resources of foreign offices.

Because only about 30,000 of 300,000 U.S. firms export, there are not very many companies involved in overseas business. But that's not to say there aren't new opportunities to be found in foreign markets, which can be researched, scouted, and entered successfully—given the right preparation. That's what the ITA does. It acts as a scout for new business by delivering direct sales leads. It locates agents and distributors for your products and helps in every way possible to see that all the details are smoothed out before that first shipment leaves your dock.

I was first introduced to the ITA through Roy Dube, an ITA international trade specialist who works out of the Chicago regional office. Dube spends a great deal of his time teaching the export business to local businessmen through community college classes, seminars, and personal visits.

Unlike a number of antiquated government operations, the ITA does database searches for private businesses looking for information on foreign companies, export agents, or other overseas trade opportunities. Because the ITA's primary mission is to support and develop U.S. business with overseas firms, it has an able marketing team that is available to the public at nominal or no charge.

As part of its overall service, the ITA accesses three databases in Dialog for its clients. Acting as a consultant, market researcher, and librarian, the ITA will determine your overseas marketing information needs, access the proper Dialog file, and retrieve anything from direct sales leads to opportunities for foreign distributorships.

THE TOP OF THE WORLD

The Trade Opportunities Program (TOP) Through its weekly TOP bulletin, the ITA culls trade leads that develop into sales leads, overseas representation opportunities, and foreign government tenders. You can subscribe to the bulletin itself for $175 a year.

A more efficient way of locating foreign sales leads, however, is by searching the two TOP files in Dialog. Along with a file called the Foreign Traders Index, TOP is a rare source of potential sales information that can be searched by four or five-digit SIC codes. Once the client has identified the product that the client represents, the type of business most likely to need it, and the country that seems most promising, the ITA specialists can prepare custom research profiles.

According to the ITA, the results of the searches are mailed out the same day they are performed. Unfortunately, the service does not have the ability to put the leads on mailing labels.

The Foreign Traders Index The ITA can generate custom export mailing lists from this Dialog database that will list specific foreign companies in the industry groups selected by the client. These mailing lists are available on gummed labels and cost from $35 on up.

The ITA also publishes international market research surveys for a given product in a specified country. The reports analyze market potential for selected products, end-users and their purchasing plans, marketing practices, and trade restrictions.

The market research surveys also attempt to pinpoint key potential buyers, government purchasing agencies, and similar organizations. The surveys also are available in ten- to fifteen-page abstracts that range in price from $9 to $10 a copy. Global market surveys that compile several company surveys are also available and vary in price.

Additionally, the ITA can aid exporters through its Agent/Distributorship Service, which will help U.S. businesses find qualified agents and distributors for products marketed overseas.

An ITA database search specialist said that searches cost from $40 to $150 with most of her clients requesting the first ten names of each list she generates. The ITA also provides a number of support services for exporters. They are:

Counseling and Seminar Program Focuses on the mechanics of exporting and individual counseling to help firms develop their export marketing plan.

New Product Information Service Publishes short descriptions of products in booklet form and distributes them to the Commerce Department's Foreign Commercial Service posts abroad. According to the ITA, this is a "good way for small firms to gain exposure abroad and test a product's reception." The charge for the service is $40.

Foreign Buyer Program The ITA will actually make appointments for you with foreign buyers visiting the U.S.

Products Marketing Service The Commerce Department's U.S. Export Development offices overseas can serve as a temporary base of operations for U.S. business executives. The service will aid executives in locating interpreters and secretaries and scheduling appointments. It will also provide advice on doing business in a specific country. There is a "modest" fee for this service.

Catalog Exhibitions Another opportunity for a small firm to promote its products overseas.

Trade Missions, Seminars, and Commercial Exhibitions
The Commerce Department will organize trade shows and act as an advisor to businesses participating in these events.

Automated Information Transfer Systems This system offers firms international marketing data on a regular basis. It provides export sales leads and information on foreign customers.

In addition to all the aforementioned services, the ITA will help businesses prepare export documentation, identify exportable products and markets, determine export prices, establish overseas distribution networks, and analyze sales strategies in priority markets. A little government involvement can be good in this case.

Costs/Information

The price the ITA charges for the database searches is $15 for a one-time access fee, $54 an hour for computer time and $.25 per lead in the six-month-old to three-year-old TOP file and $.50 per lead in the six-month-old to present file.

There are sixty U.S. Department of Commerce district offices that can supply you with information on the ITA. For more information on the location of the district office nearest you, call (202) 377-2432 or write the U.S. Dept. of Commerce, Office of Trade Information Services, P.O. Box 14207, Washington, D.C., 20044. To search the Commerce Department databases, you don't need to go through the government. They are publicly available on Dialog. Contact your information broker or librarian for more information.

COMMERCE BUSINESS DAILY

Back on the home front, the government can act not only as an advisor to U.S. businesses, but as a big customer as well. The most popular instances of government buying are probably in the defense sector where money seems to be no object when it comes to the Pentagon's wish list. But the headlines won't tell most businesses that the government as a whole has a huge ongoing need for goods and services from the private sector that get only a small amount of attention.

The smarter firms that market the government know where to find out about procurement needs and bidding. One principal source for government business opportunities is in the *Commerce Business Daily* (CBD), a publication of the U.S. Department of Commerce.

The *CBD* is a daily list of procurement invitations, contract awards, subcontracting leads, sales of surplus property, and foreign business opportunities. Actually, the *CBD* is more like a daily black-and-white magazine of government sales leads.

One way that the government announces that it wants bids to provide a service or product is through a Request for Proposal (RFP). These are notices to which businesses must respond in order to begin marketing to whatever agency has published the RFP. Since the *CBD* covers the entire range of government agencies, bureaus, departments, and other government units, the diversity of products and services needed is immense.

For instance, NASA could publish an RFP on subcontracting for its space station project. Or the Department of Agriculture could be looking for a consultant on a special plant disease. The possibilities are endless. The *CBD* is merely a clearinghouse newsletter.

How does a business market the government? One way is through a print subscription to *CBD,* which is published in Chicago. Because scanning a large, unfamiliar government publication can be like reading a document in a foreign language, there are more infocentric ways of getting sales leads from the government.

The *CBD* is a relatively popular candidate for online database vendors. The publication is loaded with good information that begs for an efficient method of locating precisely what you want. That's where online searching can save time and money.

Costs/Information

CBD is available on Dialog, (800) 3-DIALOG; SOFTSHARE (805) 683-3841; Data Resources, Inc., (617) 863-5100; and CBD Online (301) 589-8875. Every service has its own software, pricing structure, and the ability to tailor its information delivery to a company's most pressing needs.

For more information, call (312) 353-2950 or write *Commerce Business Daily* at Rm. 1304, 433 W. Van Buren St., Chicago, IL, 60607.

Generally, the online services will track down notices in the *CBD* that could develop into a sales prospect for your company. The services perform that function by locating only the notices that apply to a certain product, product group, or service. In effect, the services retrieve data only from the database daily reports of what you need. Most of the services are available through your personal computer.

For example, CBD Online, which also provides a federal marketing information service, will scan the most recent fifty-two weeks of *CBD,* list which companies were awarded contracts, and send out requests for proposals and requests for bids through the system to the issuing government office.

One distinct competitive advantage of the *CBD* online services is that they allow you to read the *CBD* before it reaches your mailbox. That can save precious time in the lengthy procurement process.

In summary, the specific applications of *CBD* online services cover:

Sales prospecting for government contracts The *CBD* covers contract awards of $25,000 or more by civil agencies; awards of $100,000 or more by military agencies; procurements for services or supplies of $5,000 or more for civil agencies, and $10,000 or more for military agencies; research and development sources sought; special notices; and surplus property sales. The notices come in the form of requests for proposals, invitations to bid, and solicitations.

Market and competitive analysis See what the government is buying, how much it is paying for it, and which companies are being awarded the contracts. It's all public information.

No matter which online service you choose, any one is more efficient than scanning outdated print editions. It's the first step in fine-tuning your electronic profit center when marketing to the government.

PINPOINT

Pinpoint, a support service for businesses involved in federal contracting, will give you the background you need to market to the government more effectively.

Costs/Information

A CACI, Inc., company, Pinpoint uses its own database of contract actions of more than $10,000 for the past four fiscal years. The company will search the database for you in a variety of formats to give you market research, competitive analysis, and an improved marketing strategy. For more information, call (800) 336-6600 or (703) 841-4600.

THE INTERNATIONAL BUSINESS CLEARINGHOUSE AND THE WORLD OF BARTERING/TRADE

If your business has no predilection for dealing with the government and wants to go it alone on the international front, there is an electronic network in place for international trade and bartering.

The International Business Clearinghouse (IBC) serves its clients via Western Union's EasyLink FYI service. IBC, operated by Barter Worldwide, Inc., actually lists goods or services on the system. These items can be bartered for other goods or services, a potentially rewarding activity considering the cash flow and savings advantages.

IBC is organized on EasyLink by five sections:

Barter/Countertrade IBC handles any transaction.

Bids and Buying Companies request bids from vendors in specific categories.

Inventory/Liquidation Enables companies to list merchandise for sale.

Sellers Lists product lines and services.

Media Companies can purchase advertising in exchange for goods or services.

According to Mike Jeffries, president of Barter Worldwide, bartering is a fast-growing business that involves sixty-five percent of Fortune 500 companies.

Companies typically list goods or services valued at $100,000 per item for six months and are charged $150. IBC also charges a transaction fee ranging from six percent to ten percent of the value of each sale made.

The most infocentric advantage of IBC is that it's linked to EasyLink's Telex network, so that companies on the service can communicate and transact business through the popular Telex system. There are three Telex options on EasyLink (see Chapter Four on online utilities), so it would not be difficult to use the system.

Bartering can be ideal for companies wishing to preserve cash flow and obtain goods or services at a discount. For example, a long-distance telephone company can trade $1 million in long-distance service for the same amount of advertising. Since there is no disbursement of funds, the company retains $1 million in cash reserves. Also, since every transaction is done on the wholesale level, there are no distribution or marketing costs in many cases, Jeffries said.

The IBC is additionally instrumental in gaining customers with whom you might not ordinarily do business because of cash flow problems, in liquidating excess inventory, in making "bargain" purchases, and in allowing you to get money out of countries that won't let you withdraw currency. The service would be useful for business people involved in:

Purchasing management A wide variety of goods and services are listed at relatively good prices.

Sales prospecting A unique sales and marketing tool that allows greater flexibility in marketing without traditional promotional or advertising costs.

Financial management Preserves cash flow and obtains needed goods and services.

Costs/Information

For more information on IBC, call IBC at (213) 641-1000, Telex at 466807, or EasyLink at (201) 825-5223.

9

ADVANCED APPLICATIONS

- EXECUTIVE INFORMATION SYSTEMS
- CD-ROM: COMPACT DATABASE INFORMATION
- E-MAIL/PRIVATE DATABASE SERVICES
- ADP AUTOMAIL
- BRS
- COMPUSERVE
- DELPHI/GROUPLINK
- GE QUICK-COMM
- GTE TELEMAIL
- DIALCOM
- ORBIT
- THE SOURCE
- DATABASE APPLICATIONS FOR RETAILING AND PUBLIC INFORMATION
- ELECTRONIC BANKING FOR PERSONAL COMPUTERS
- COVIDEA
- CHASE MANHATTAN BANK
- CITIBANK
- MANUFACTURERS HANOVER TRUST (MHT)
- OTHER TELEBANKING VENDORS
- REGIONAL TELEBANKING SERVICES
- THE FUTURE OF TELEBANKING
- THE FUTURE

131

There are a number of promising developments in the online database and videotex field worth noting in the process of becoming infocentric. The following products and services—in various stages of development—are worth considering to enhance your electronic profit centers.

EXECUTIVE INFORMATION SYSTEMS

A key development for corporate professionals is the *executive information system* (EIS). This system searches databases and makes the information available to the executive with a computer terminal, thus eliminating the need for the executive to search online databases directly or hire someone to do it. The EIS configuration uses micro- and minicomputers to select, direct, and network online information directly to decisionmakers. That way, they don't have to search databases at all. The system will search for them, picking out timely information on mergers and acquisitions, company reports, competitive intelligence, and trade news.

The most visible benefit of the EIS is that it saves time. It can swiftly relay critical information on the competition, merger and acquisition targets and suitors, industry news, and intercompany activities.

Although only a handful of companies, such as Firestone Tire and Rubber and Gillette, have these systems, thousands of companies are considering them. The systems provide an efficient way to channel data by automating information acquisition.

CD-ROM: COMPACT DATABASE INFORMATION

Another way of eliminating the information "middleman" is to have important external databases in-house. One of the ways databases can be directly accessed by personal computers is through *compact disk–read only memory* (CD-ROM). A compact disk the size of a saucer is loaded with about 400 megabytes (i.e., 400 million bytes) of information and is read by a laser beam on a CD player similar to the units that produce crisp digital stereo sound. The disk can be searched like an online database.

CD-ROM's greatest advantage over online databases is that you don't pay for connect or telecommunications time. You pay an annual flat fee. The databases stored on compact disks can be read by special devices that connect directly to personal computers. You can own an extensive database on companies in a particular industry and access it easily at any time. You pay for the information—and special equipment to access it—on a yearly or quarterly basis.

The drawbacks of CD-ROM, as of this writing, are connected with price and inflexibility. A CD-ROM drive for a PC sells for around $700 and up (the cost of an entire PC), you can only read a limited number of CDs, and there is a yearly "subscription fee" from $4,000 to $20,000. Part of the high cost is due to the process that transfers the information onto the disk. It costs about $7,000 to "master" the information onto a compact disk. And once the information is etched onto a CD, it is static. Unlike a floppy disc, CDs are currently unable to receive new information with available equipment—hence the "read-only" label. The software used to search the databases is also less flexible than its online counterparts. Timely information (from a day to several weeks old) simply isn't available on CDs yet. So if you need an updated CD, the vendor will simply sell you another one.

Of the companies that currently publish CD-ROM databases, all require a special CD-ROM drive to search the databases and some training. Most will include the drive as part of a subscription. Although CD-ROM databases aren't likely to displace online databases as timely, comprehensive sources of information in the near future, they are worth considering for limited needs. The following are the major CD-ROM business information vendors:

Datext, Inc.
444 Washington St.
Woburn, MA 01801
Telephone: (617) 938-6667

The company's CD/Corporate database covers more than 10,000 publicly-traded U.S. companies. Financial information and analysts' reports are included in the company records. A $19,600 yearly subscription includes a disk drive and monthly updates.

Disclosure
5161 River Road
Bethesda, MD 20816
Telephone: (301) 951-1300

Produced by the same company that features public company and demographic information on online databases, Compact Disclosure contains financial information on 11,000 public companies. A $4,500 annual subscription includes hardware and four quarterly-updated disks. Noncommercial rates are also available.

Information Access Company
11 Davis Dr.
Belmont, CA 94002
Telephone: (415) 591-2333; (800) 227-8431

Information Access Company's InfoTrac database is an index to 900 publications; the InfoTrac II database tracks 400 general-interest magazines. A yearly lease costs $4,500.

E-MAIL / PRIVATE DATABASE SERVICES

If you are currently using online databases on a regular basis, you might eventually have a need to create your own "private database" and access it through an electronic mail network. For large organizations, this could make communications and information distribution over great distances much more efficient. This section explains how electronic mail (E-mail) and private databases can make an organization more infocentric.

Before you consider whether you need electronic mail or a private database, though, it's important to understand the evolution of these services. One of the first companies that helped make E-mail and videotex possible on a large scale was the General Telephone and Electronics Corporation (GTE), which started its Telenet network to serve a growing group of computer users who needed to send data over long distances but found it extremely expensive to use the existing transcontinental long-distance network.

Telenet is a "packet-switching" network, or a telephone network that takes bunches of telephone messages locally and switches them into a larger network for wider distribution. What this means is that videotex users who live in, say, California, and want to use a service like The Source, which has its main computers on the East Coast, would have to dial into a local number in California and be essentially charged for a local call plus The Source's "connect time" rates. If the user wanted to dial directly to Columbus, Ohio, it would cost a lot more. Thus it is packet switching that makes online database access economical. It can be argued that the growing cost advantage of packet-switching networks combined with a legion of home computer enthusiasts fueled the growth of videotex. Now business is stoking the fire under videotex's growth.

The field of companies offering packet-switched networks has also grown. Tymshare (Tymnet), Dialog (Dialnet), Mead Data Central (MeadNet), and Compuserve all have their own networks, primarily designed to cater to their own group of database subscribers. As telecommunications technology improves, the field should become even more crowded.

Packet-switching networks are the nerve centers that make data communications and videotex compatible. They provide a relatively cheap route for electronic mail, private networks, and other corporate videotex functions. Besides database access, the most prevalent use of the networks is for electronic mail. Although E-mail is still more expensive than conventional methods, it can ease some business communications problems.

What is Electronic Mail?

Although E-mail was developed before videotex, both came from the same original source. E-mail is a feature common to some mainframes and minicomputers, as well as a few microcomputers. It is mainly used to talk from terminal to terminal or, more specifically, from user to user. Users are given "mailboxes," which consist of their identification (ID) name or number and a place within the computer to store the messages. The messages can be retrieved whenever a user logs on and chooses to read them.

One related E-mail service is called an electronic bulletin board. This feature is a way of "posting" or reading messages for a certain group. There are thousands of bulletin boards that cater to personal computer users throughout the country. Many of the specialty bulletin boards available on the online utilities and consumer videotex services are called *special interest groups* (SIGs). These services tailor their computer space to groups sharing a common interest like photography or sailing. The same concept applies to business applications. Bulletin boards are, however, a small part of the videotex communications universe and may not be accessible by certain E-mail services. Many of them serve local audiences. They may be accessed through an online utility or consumer videotex service or set up in private or corporate videotex systems in conjunction with E-mail.

E-Mail Cost Savings

For businesses and organizations, the best reason to use E-mail is volume cost savings. According to Presentation Consultants (PC), a New York consulting firm that specializes in E-mail studies, volume savings can be significant.

In one PC study, the firm compared E-mail costs to those of several overnight delivery services. Using E-mail to deliver one two-page letter/memo per week resulted in annual savings of "$81,380 over Federal Express next-day delivery; $35,620 over MCI Mail next-day delivery; and $16,380 over Western Union's Mailgram."

The consultants also found notable cost-per-unit savings in using E-mail over courier services. While the Federal Express cost-per-unit (of the same two-page memo) was about $10, it was about $2.17 per unit on Dialcom's E-mail service. E-mail was also found to have cost advantages over conventional electronic messaging services such as telex.

Who Offers E-Mail Services?

The majority of videotex systems offer E-mail capabilities that vary depending upon the size of the system and number of users involved. Compuserve, which has more than 250,000 users, has an extensive E-mail system that makes it possible for every user on the system to talk to any other user, provided that they know the ID of the user to whom they want to communicate. (Compuserve provides a list of user IDs to Compuserve subscribers only.) Smaller E-mail systems may reach only the total number of terminal users within a company. In short, E-mail is offered by:

Systems vendors If you buy a system from IBM, DEC, Honeywell, or any of the other major vendors, E-mail is a part of the basic package. If not, it can usually be provided with the proper software.

E-Mail services These companies may offer nothing but E-mail through a national system that might connect you to other communications services such as telex. Western Union, MCI Mail, GE, RCA, and GTE are the major forces in this area. These firms may also be able to set up E-mail networks for an entire company to link branch offices.

Online utilities or videotex services Compuserve, The Source, and Delphi all have E-mail systems of their own that come with their basic package of services.

Private networks/database, videotex, or closed user groups All are different names for the same thing: the combination of a private company database or electronic bulletin board with an E-mail network. BRS, Compuserve, The Source, Delphi, ORBIT, and other database vendors or utilities are active in this area. These services may be highly customized to an individual organization's needs.

E-Mail and Private Database Applications

The ability to distribute a variety of information over a great distance is one obvious advantage of E-mail. But, then, so can a telephone network. What makes E-mail gain that "extra yard"? The following are some special functions of E-mail and private databases:

An alternative to the post office/mailroom Although E-mail doesn't pretend to replace the efficiency of the mailed letter or document, it can reduce the overall mail load. Additionally, significant cost/volume reductions can be realized by using E-mail. If you need to avoid the three or four days it takes to receive a first-class letter, E-mail can accomplish the task in a few minutes. It may cost up to

110 percent more, but the savings in time and productivity could add up. These services also turn nearly any personal computer or terminal with a modem into an international communications device. For time-sensitive material that has to reach any number of people in a short period of time, E-mail is ideal.

A great message taker Unlike brief telephone messages taken by somebody else that tell you little, an E-mail message is an entire set of ideas written out and stored for you. You can read as much as you want at your convenience.

A timesaver You consume a lot of wasted time in playing "telephone tag." This modern ritual involves an all-too-familiar volley of noncommunication played by people who have little interest in your message. E-mail ends the game by allowing you to respond, comprehend, and retrieve a message at any time you log onto a system, even in the middle of the night, if possible. It saves time because it caters to your schedule.

Teleconferencing Some E-mail/videotex systems will allow a group of people to participate in teleconferencing, with all the participants sitting at their own terminals no matter where they are in the world, and carry on a conservation via telephone lines—with words becoming text on a video screen. This saves the expense and scheduling problems involved in gathering several different people in one place at one time.

A "frequent flyer" program The more an organization uses E-mail, the more it saves. The fact that you don't have to fly personnel all over the country (or world) to take meetings is one savings component. Another is the reduction in nonproductive time spent in airports, taxis, hotel lobbies, and smoky lounges listening to bad singers entertaining people who didn't want to be there in the first place.

Reducing net travel expenses may make a good system pay for itself.

A management tool The cost and time savings of E-mail usage give executives more time to pool information and make informed decisions. They also encourage more communication within an organization by making memos more immediate, comprehensive, and interactive. For example, sales people can send or receive sales data or leads while they are working in the field.

A clerical tool Typists, stenos, administrators, secretaries, and clerks will come to use E-mail even more than executives because it gives them more time for more important tasks. A good E-mail system will allow a user to copy and distribute a message to any number of other users within the system. It really takes the burden off that belabored photocopy machine.

A distribution/traffic manager Nearly all the E-mail systems described in this book allow you to send multiple copies of your message or business form to virtually any number of persons on a predesignated list. And all this work is done with little labor and cost.

An international communicator The best E-mail systems connect to telex services, Mailgram, Cablegram, electronic letters, E-COM, bulletin boards, and databases. The Telex network alone can reach 1.6 million subscribers worldwide. An electronic letter sends a message from your computer to the distribution office of the E-mail service, where it is printed out and dropped in the mail to the addressee.

Disadvantages of E-Mail

What makes E-mail a less-universal mode of communication than voice telephone circuits is that different E-mail systems are not compatible. They are, therefore, relatively useless unless the party you are sending the message to has an ID on the same E-mail service with which you are sending the message.

For instance, an MCI Mail user cannot send an electronic message to someone on Compuserve's EasyPlex service and vice versa. However, that same MCI Mail user would have the option of reaching the person not on MCI Mail by sending a $4 MCI Mail letter, which is an electronic message that is printed out and dropped in the mail for first-class delivery.

The problem of E-mail incompatibility is, to a large degree, typical of the computer industry in general: the marketplace is a poor guiding force in getting all the vendors to adopt one set of standards. Although several groups are pushing for one E-mail standard as this book goes to press, that development is years away.

E-mail also cannot be utilized for sending large parcels, documents, packages, and, in most cases, graphics. But, for smaller messages, E-mail can be ideal.

Some technology naysayers also argue that E-mail may increase nonproductive time and reduce interpersonal contact, since E-mail requires a smaller outlay of effort and clerical support. Additionally, as with any communications system, there is also the increased chance of message loss and system breakdown. Any organization that is extremely dependent on E-mail could be crippled if its system goes down.

There is, in addition, a security issue involved. No matter what ID/password scheme is used, some system outside your organization must do the processing. Amid stories of credit computers being broken into, the security dilemma has not been totally resolved. Although there have never been any reports about *any* security problems with E-mail, there is nothing to suggest that E-mail is tamper-proof. But this problem is sure to gain more notoriety as more E-mail users come into the fold. At this writing, however, there is no substantial evidence against using E-mail for security reasons.

For a small volume of messages, E-mail is also one of the most expensive ways of communicating. However, high-volume users could realize significant cost savings.

Choosing an E-Mail/Communications Vendor

Choosing a communications system depends upon the type of messages to be sent and medium to be used. The services can be categorized as:

Basic message services GE's Quick-Comm, GTE's Telemail, and ADP Automail are tailored for corporate users with heavy E-mail requirements.

Value-added E-mail systems MCI Mail, also known as a "public access E-mail" service, goes one step beyond basic E-mail. MCI, with its MCI Mail letters, will take electronic messages, print them out, and drop them in the mail. The service will even promise four-hour delivery of messages at an additional cost.

E-Mail plus teleconferencing and public online databases This is where the utilities like Compuserve, The Source, Dialcom, and Western Union's EasyLink come in. All have basic E-mail services; however, they also have databases that feature everything from news to stock quotations. Compuserve, The Source, and Dialcom have teleconferencing features. EasyLink offers a research service, telex, mailgram, electronic letters, and an FYI news service.

Private networks and databases All the utilities plus BRS and ORBIT feature this service, which will take an organization's data, store them on the vendor's computers, make them accessible by telephone network, and customize them to include bulletin boards, order entry, E-mail, and other specified company information. In effect, such databases are creating "mini-utilities" that can be accessed by only the organization that ordered them.

Advanced E-Mail Services

The utilities offer an array of services ranging from information retrieval to private networks. Naturally, these additional communications options cost more than basic E-mail and allow more flexibility. Teleconferencing, for example, allows several participants to talk back and forth by typing messages on a video screen in a "live" format, as if they were holding a conversation via Citizens' Band radio. In fact, one of the services is called "CB."

E-mail typically has some delay built into it. The teleconferencing services on the utilities are a far cry from a telephone conference call or video conference because teleconferencing may be open to anyone using a "channel" on the utility, allowing anyone to participate in the computer conversation. However, their ability to attract spontaneous conversations among users with similar interests does serve a purpose: it can lead to fresh insights from unexpected sources.

For even greater customization, the utilities and some other database vendors offer private networks, which allow any one organization to create its own databases and communications networks. The basic E-mail services do not do this. Private networks, unlike basic E-mail, are more like true videotex applications because they combine data storage and retrieval, communications and ease of use for a common group of users.

When to Use a Private Network/Database

It is really a fairly simple matter to determine when to use a private network or database. Most private network set-ups generally charge $5,000 and up to create a private network/database. (The terms *network, database,* and *private database* are interchangeable.) This fee usually includes the use of a remote computer and a communications system (typically E-mail) and the creation of a customized database that all the users on the network can access at any time. This database could include anything from company policy manuals to bulletin boards on sales seminars. This is an external electronic publishing application that grew out of time-sharing services (i.e., using somebody else's computer for your data processing).

Although any company can start its own in-house private network, an organization needs the videotex hardware and software to do this, which means an expenditure that may run into six figures.

Private networks are not only useful for any size organization that can't justify the cost of an in-house videotex system, but they are also a great bargain. The initial price of $5,000 is probably less than the cost of two personal computer workstations with hard drives, modems, printers, and software.

Vendors

The vendors profiled in the following sections can provide one or more of the aforementioned communications services. Some are only electronic messaging services. Others have ventured into private networks. All have established reputations in either communications or database creation and vending. The utilities have made their name in consumer videotex and have only really begun marketing to businesses in the past three years. The following service profiles are meant to provide an overview of services and pricing. They are not in any way intended to be technical or qualitative evaluations of the services. All prices are subject to change.

Charges for communication services are based on (1)

"connect time" to the service, which is either a flat rate or based on each 1,000 characters used, (2) telecommunications time that the packet-switching network charges, and (3) set-up charges, usually for the private creation and maintenance costs.

In choosing a vendor, consider the following questions and answers:

1. Q: Do I need simple E-mail messaging or a network that will link offices and provide databases for organizational access?

   A: If the first part of the question was yes, you need an E-mail/messaging vendor, most of which carry additional services like telex. If the first and second parts were yes, then you might need a communications service and a private network/database.

2. Q: Are my E-mail/communications needs large or small?

   A: Vendors who handle large-scale communications needs are noted below. Generally, your communications needs are large scale if you have a large, computer-literate organization that will use an E-mail system or database service.

3. Q: How do I know if my organization needs a private network/database?

   A: You need one if you find it necessary to link offices with E-mail or create a specialized database for your organization and have any member of your organization access it from any point in the country. To justify the cost of the network, compare the monthly costs of conventional printing, mailing, and telephoning to the expected costs of the electronic vendor's proposed scheme.

The addresses and telephone numbers of the vendors discussed in the following sections are listed in Appendix C.

ADP AUTOMAIL

ADP Automail is offered through ADP's Autonet, a packet-switching network. ADP has been a major provider of business information services for more than ten years. As one would expect, Autonet is an E-mail system tailored to large-scale corporate use. This is one of the "basic" E-mail services that does little else beyond messaging.

Costs

Automail costs $100 per month per account and is also accessible through Tymnet, Telenet, or WATS. The fee structure beyond that is extremely complicated. However, there are $5-per-hour surcharges for Tymnet and Telenet and $18-per-hour surcharges for WATS. There are no telecommunications costs for subscribers using the Autonet network.

For heavy, basic messaging needs, industry analysts point to Automail as one of the most cost-efficient E-mail services. It also gets high ratings on ease of use. The system does little else besides E-mail, although it can support bulletin boards, electronic filing, address lists, telex access, and online assistance.

BRS

With prior experience gained from its BRS, BRS/After Dark, and BRS/BRKTHRU services, BRS Information Technologies is a respected database vendor and provider of database services. BRS databases currently cater to the scientific, engineering, medical, and academic communities. Its clients are well known, with large-scale operations. BRS is, therefore, an expert in large-scale information needs.

Through its Private Database service, BRS will "mount" an organization's database on its own computers.

This means that BRS will organize the database, store it, and provide the software to search and access it. A sister service, called the Supported Public File Service, makes the database accessible by users outside of an organization.

One of the most noteworthy examples of BRS's development efforts is a database maintained by JA Micropublishing, Inc., which makes available more than 35,000 corporate and industry research reports issued by major investment firms. BRS was instrumental in making JA's database publicly available. Other BRS clients include The American Hospital Association and the National Center for Research in Vocational Education.

Costs

For either of its database services, BRS charges an initial development fee of $20,000 and an ongoing database maintenance fee of $13,800 for the second year of the development. Additional development and consulting fees start at $1,000 per day. BRS's specialty is database development and information retrieval, especially if a company's prospective database is on magnetic tape or machine-readable format. Its private and public databases are accessible through the Telenet, Tymnet, or Uninet networks.

COMPUSERVE

As one of the oldest and most successful consumer videotex utilities, Compuserve has been actively marketing its services to the business community with its Business information service, Executive information service, and Interchange (Compuserve's private network service). The first two services have a generous array of online databases that feature stock quotations, demographic information, airline schedules and bookings, company information, and the InfoPlex electronic mail system.

With more than 250,000 subscribers, Compuserve is the leading videotex service in the U.S. The company, which originally started as a time-sharing specialist, also offers 400 databases in its Consumer information service.

Although the core of its subscriber base primarily uses the consumer service, Compuserve offers both E-mail and private network development services. All these services share Compuserve's own telecommunications network, which is also the network for InfoPlex. Compuserve's E-mail strengths were multiplied early in 1986 when it announced a joint agreement with MCI Mail to link the two E-mail systems, creating the largest such system in the U.S.

Clients for InfoPlex include a computer-manufacturing company, government agencies, a major snack food manufacturer, and a large pharmaceutical firm. The former company uses InfoPlex to connect regional sales offices, which receive sales reports as soon as they are published—far superior to the three- to four-day wait by mail.

Interchange, which Compuserve bills as a private business videotex service, "tailors databases to a client's particular needs," according to Rich Baker of Compuserve. Companies can use the system for price schedules, inventory availability, newsletters, sales reports, job listings, and executive status reports.

One example of a communications network being used for private videotex is Plastiserv. Although it is not a service developed through Interchange, Plastiserv (an information network for the plastics industry) uses Compuserve's packet-switching network. Industry professionals can access the system to use E-mail and scan product guides, decision reports, excerpts from the trade journal *Plastics World,* buyers' guides, and industry news. Like most private networks, Plastiserv bills its customers for connect time, which runs from $35 to $60 an hour. It also charges a one-time $75 subscription fee. It is a fairly easy-to-use system that communicates to an entire industry with usable business information on suppliers and companies with specialties and, additionally, provides an electronic industry newsletter.

Costs

A service developed by Compuserve's Interchange staff would cost an initial $5,000 and would support ten simultaneous users. InfoPlex is included in the basic service. When clients sign a contract for Interchange services, they pay the $5,000 for a three-month pilot. Beyond that period, Baker notes, different price schedules are involved that mean a greater or smaller expenditure depending upon the size of the database and other support services needed. The trial period is a good way for a business to determine if it needs a private videotex service. Compuserve's expertise in this area is considerable.

DELPHI/GROUPLINK

As one of the newest entrants into business videotex, Delphi is also the smallest in terms of numbers of subscribers (about 20,000). But what it lacks in sheer numbers, it makes up for in its ability to recognize the importance of the business market's hand in the growth of videotex. Originally started in Cambridge, Massachusetts, by Wes Kussmaul as an online encyclopedia, Delphi is owned and operated by the privately-held General Videotex Corporation.

Delphi found out early on in the consumer videotex fray that the business and professional users were the market of the future. Several special interest groups on Delphi that cater to professional groups are thriving.

What makes Delphi an even more rounded service are links to other electronic mail services on Compuserve, The Source, and Dialcom. Delphi also has links with Telex and the Postal Service's E-COM electronic letter service.

According to Chip Mathes, a Grouplink product manager, Grouplink is capable of providing customized applications for groups or associations with specialized information needs. He cites the example of a performing artists network in which booking agents maintain a database of available acts and dates.

The people running Delphi are interested in making their services as simple and accessible as possible. The company appears to be fully able to implement new ideas into Grouplink and will continue to be a potent force in private videotex.

Costs

In private videotex, Delphi offers its Grouplink service as a custom private network. For a one-time $5,000 set-up fee that includes user training, Grouplink can combine E-mail, teleconferencing, cataloging, file management, bulletin boards, directories, polling, news services, newsletters, and travel services. Delphi connect times for Grouplink are among the lowest in the industry, ranging from $.30/minute to $.15/minute. In addition to those charges are several support-related fees.

GE QUICK-COMM

Just as the name implies, General Electric's Quick-Comm is more or less just that—fast communications. Quick-Comm uses the same vast, worldwide communications network that GE's GEISCO computer information system has been using for years. Actually, Quick-Comm is but one of many integrated data-processing services GE offers in its Mark III program, which caters to large-scale corporate data-processing needs. However, Quick-Com—the electronic mail service—is available to any size business. Since Quick-Comm is a heavy-duty communications network, it is better understood by data-processing professionals because the system is capable of transferring massive amounts of data as well as performing simpler applications such as accessing Telex.

The capabilities of Quick-Comm also extend beyond communications. Electronic mail can be forwarded to another party, copied, or stored in GE computers. Quick-Comm even allows for coding of messages from person to person for security purposes.

Costs

The complex pricing for Quick-Comm can be even more baffling than that of EasyLink because it is based on the amount of information sent—from $.35/300 characters to $.80/page for 3,000 characters or more. There is no monthly minimum or subscription fee, but that's largely a moot point considering that GE designed Quick-Comm for high-volume corporate use. And, as a major data-processing service company, GE also offers complete software and hardware sales support.

GTE TELEMAIL

Telemail was a natural outgrowth of GTE's Telenet packet-switching network. As a pioneer in packet-switching services, GTE's technology made videotex possible on a national scale. When other telecommunications concerns followed GTE into the business, GTE suddenly was forced to be the innovator and leader.

Although the services Telemail provides are not nearly as diverse as those of EasyLink, it has some respectable offerings and a sizable customer base. It also connects with a Canadian electronic mail service.

The service provides electronic mail, telex, Telemail-Xpress (electronic letter) and an overnight delivery service. For corporate customers, GTE also provides a public data network service that will essentially link computers in separate locations. Although this offering may or may not be considered a form of videotex because it primarily involves data-processing professionals, it is one of the value-added services GTE provides that makes videotex possible through telecommunications connections.

Costs

Telemail costs subscribers $100 (a one-time fee) and $4 to $14/hour for connect time, depending on the hour of day. In addition to a $140 account charge, there is also a $500 monthly minimum after the first three months of usage.

In GTE's own words, "Telemail was conceived as an improved communications vehicle for upper-level management." Because it plays in the same league as GE, Fortune 1000 companies appear to be GTE's prime market.

DIALCOM

On first glance, Dialcom's cornucopia of services is like a combination of research department, clerical pool, wire room, PC workstation, and word-processing clerk bundled together inside a personal computer. Dialcom has designed a full-service communications product that, although it may not have a crystal-clear identity, is competent in any of a dozen separate areas.

Unlike any other competing service, Dialcom offers online word processing. For example, that means a user in an airport using a portable computer can type and send an electronic letter back to the home office. In addition to its own electronic mail service, Dialcom also has the ability to send telexes, electronic letters, mailgrams, telegrams, and electronic (customized) forms and to perform teleconferencing. Online-database access to Dow Jones News Retrieval, UPI news and stocks, Dialog, and Official Airline Guide is also available at extra charge. A feature called WPMail can even link two word processors for electronic mail messaging.

In addition to its international connection to databases and communications services, Dialcom can provide electronic publishing that will create for an individual organization databases that can be accessed through the Dialcom network. As an option to the basic Dialcom package, this service can start at $19.50 an hour to access. Development costs are additional. Simpler services like special interest group bulletin boards can also be developed at additional cost, provided that there are enough users to justify the cost of the service.

Like most companies that are in the communications business, Dialcom keeps a tight rein on naming specific companies that are customers. One good example, though, is a food distribution company that equipped its field salesmen with portable terminals to get timely reports on store inventories and product orders, thereby "increasing the efficiency of its production scheduling and delivery."

Costs

Pricing for Dialcom's E-mail runs from $14/hour to $30/hour. Dialcom clearly has the corporate customer in mind, since it charges a $100 monthly minimum. Usage fees are based on the service used and get more complicated depending on which and how many services are accessed. Volume discounts are available.

ORBIT

Building on its strengths as a leading database provider to the scientific and technical community, Pergamon's ORBIT division offers a private file service.

The approach that this service takes is similar to that of BRS. Its experts organize your records or documents into a database on their computers for easy access. Their support is complete, since they provide software, hardware, and technical assistance.

Costs

Pricing for Private File starts at $5,000 for initial file design and loading of the first 10,000 records. Users are charged an additional $40/hour to access the database. There is also a whole range of service-related charges that are incurred for tasks like updating and reloading. A private file-testing program is available for $3,000. Training is provided at $350 per seminar.

The ORBIT search service division has gained extensive experience in offering databases to public or private organizations. One of the many databases available on ORBIT is called INSPEC, which covers current technological developments in computers and telecommunications.

Like many of its competitors, ORBIT is extremely data-processing oriented; that is, it can more easily deal with data-processing or MIS professionals than with computer novices. However, it has shown ample ability in putting together private databases.

THE SOURCE

The Source, owned by the Reader's Digest Association, is one of the kindly grandfathers of videotex. Its consumer service was originally embraced by computer enthusiasts. In recent years, though, it has been actively courting the business community.

Like the private database offerings of the other utilities, The Source is leasing its computer and telecommunications network to any group that needs its own database, E-mail service, bulletin board, or online newsletter. And, also like its rivals, The Source can offer teleconferencing, electronic surveys, news, stock quotations, and a full range of online databases.

According to Nancy Beckman, a Source spokeswoman, one Source private network is being used by a "major computer retail chain to communicate between franchises financial figures, corporate events, industry news, and sales reports."

Based on price alone, The Source's private networks appear to be a good value. At this writing, though, it is too soon to tell how The Source is faring in the development and service departments.

Costs

What separates The Source from the rest of the industry is its simple, cost-efficient pricing schedule. Private networks can be created for $5,000, which includes software, set-up, training, electronic mail, and user support. The Source also promises to have the network up and running in about thirty to forty-five days. That figure will vary depending on the size of the service to be implemented.

DATABASE APPLICATIONS FOR RETAILING AND PUBLIC INFORMATION

Another application of databases and CD-ROM technology allows nearly any provider of information access to the public without human intervention. If you know how effectively databases can work in information retrieval, you can extend that thinking to the "dispensing" of information as well. Several companies specialize in building whole systems for dispensing information around a single database. In this medium, the public has direct access to the database. They needn't know anything about databases or computers since they retrieve the information in special kiosks equipped with video screens, speakers, and keyboards.

Generally known as *interactive video*, this marriage of CD-ROM to databases combines a CD-ROM/videodisk player, a database, and a kiosk that contains a video screen, stereo speakers, and a keyboard. Users are able to walk up to a kiosk in a shopping mall or other public setting, select product/service information, and see audio-video displays on that product or service. Some kiosks even allow users to insert a credit card to order merchandise.

Interactive video has numerous business applications in retailing, public access information, merchandising, and corporate training and information dissemination. This section primarily focuses on interactive retailing.

Although the overall efficacy of interactive retailing has yet to be fully researched, it is already in use by companies such as GM, Merck, Marshall Fields, and Florsheim. Florsheim, for example, employs interactive kiosks in its shoe stores to dispense product information. Though it doesn't use CD-ROM, GM's Buick division is testing interactive systems to distribute product information at dealerships. This medium is also used by corporations to distribute information in public areas. Banks, for example, are using interactive kiosks to display information on banking services and investment products such as Certificates of Deposit.

Interactive kiosks may also be found in hotel lobbies and airports. Many of the kiosks serve as guides to cities, restaurants, and nightlife. In retail and corporate settings, they are popular dispensers of information, since they are perceived as "friendly" and "visual." For a multitude of public users, interactive kiosks can deliver a message to nearly anyone—and with a technology that is nonintimidating. There are several vendors that specialize in this medium, which is gaining momentum as a new way of presenting information.

How the Medium Works

Interactive video typically combines a computer, a compact disk (CD) player, often what is known as a "touchscreen," and, in certain cases, a connection to a central computer. When a kiosk is capable of telecommunicating with another computer, it ranks as a videotex device. At the core of the kiosk's brain are several million pieces of information that are stored on the CD player. The CD, or "laser disk" player, is able to read this information via a laser beam that scans tracks on a shiny plastic disk similar to the way a phonograph needle follows the grooves of a record to transmit sound through an amplifier and speakers.

Unlike the mechanical/electronic process employed in a phonograph, however, a CD player scans patterns of light that are then interpreted as data, audio signals, or video images. In other words, the laser "reads" the disk the way a phonograph stylus would track a vinyl record, except that a CD can hold thousands of times more information than a record and can combine sound and video.

CD technology, also found in the popular CD players in stereo and video stores, is capable of storing an entire database of information, separate audiovisual sales pitches for hundreds of products, and the instructions for the user. In the case of the Marshall Fields kiosk, manufactured by ByVideo, Inc., of Sunnyvale, California, the system was able not only to give friendly instructions by a recorded voice, but it could also take orders, since it had a built-in device that would "read" the magnetic strip on credit cards. Once the order was processed by another computer, the kiosk could also arrange delivery of the desired merchandise. In a sense, the kiosk has adopted the role of salesperson, cashier, and warehouse clerk.

Applications

It is possible to observe the noncommercial cousin of electronic retailing—public access videotex—in a number of highly visible places from coast to coast. You can find kiosks in LaGuardia Airport in New York and in hotels in San Francisco. The kiosks serve as interactive video guides to the respective metropolitan areas. In Dallas, kiosks in the Galleria shopping center and the Infomart convention center serve as directories to services and building occupants. On the Galleria system, users can choose categories like restaurants and shoe stores to find specific store locations in the huge indoor shopping mall. Similar retailing systems are capable of using similar powers of information retrieval and have the added ability of processing transactions.

Interactive video is also being used as a training tool and banking-information medium. These applications, which do not usually require telecommunications, are also based on videodisk hardware. Typically, a great deal of information can be stored on a videodisk for portable presentation. The use of interactive video in audiovisual presentations and corporate training is a business unto itself.

Why It's Interactive

Another one of the elements of interactive video or electronic retailing is the touchscreen, which bypasses a keyboard by allowing the user to touch choice areas directly on the screen, which is sensitive to the heat of a single finger. A touch signals the computer to move to another part of a programmed menu. For example, on a menu that displays "shoes, socks, and belts," a user can touch an area on the screen corresponding to "shoes." A new menu would then appear that would specify either "men's," "ladies'," or "children's" shoes. After that choice was made, menus would appear asking the user to select a particular style of shoe. A video would then display either a fixed or moving image of the item selected. Music and voiceover could accompany the displays in a "minicommercial" format complete with pitch and further instructions on how to order through the kiosk.

Advantages of the Medium

For the retailer, the kiosk has freed salespeople to work with more customers, allowed companies to present a certain range of merchandise in an attractive presentation, and given shoppers the ability to make a better-informed choice in a shorter period of time. Other clear advantages of interactive video are:

Economy Once the retailer has paid for the kiosk and necessary software development, the rest of the costs are predictable and fixed. Through a steady sales volume, a kiosk can pay for itself.

Selectivity It is a good medium to move the type of hard goods that do not need close visual inspection. It can also be used to promote slower-moving goods, specialty items, higher-priced merchandise, and discounted goods that need to be highlighted.

Focus Because it isolates one set of images at a time, it restricts the customers' attention to a given range of merchandise. There are no "competing" floor displays in the small space of a kiosk.

Space Savings Selling through a kiosk essentially augments limited store space. A greater variety of goods can be displayed where they can't be stocked.

Improved Accounting Because the kiosk is guided by a computer, it imposes inventory control and provides the retailer with an exact accounting of what's being viewed and what's being sold.

Accuracy All the information you program into the machine is up to date. Prices appear next to the product on the screen and can't be switched. This may cut down on shrinkage (loss or theft).

Efficiency Customers can spend as long as they like previewing products without tying up a salesperson in an interaction that may not result in a sale.

Informativeness Because the kiosk is collecting data, it will tell the retailer which items are being sold, which are being browsed, how long certain items are viewed, and how they could be packaged. In short, a kiosk is its own market research team.

Flexibility More products can be featured on the system than can be effectively merchandised on the sales floor. More details about specific products can also be stored in the system, enhancing sales information capabilities.

Interactivity Kiosks draw traffic because they are audiovisual devices. The power of the small screen in any setting should never be underestimated. It's similar to watching television.

The Investment in a New Medium

Electronic retailing is something so new that almost no background research existed at the time of publication to verify or refute any claims about the efficacy of the kiosk as a selling machine. Many companies were involved primarily in trial phases as this book went to press. There simply were no figures available on how well these machines were selling, if they were any more effective than human salespeople, or if they were worth the investment. Naysayers asserted that the kiosks would be more threatening than friendly because of their high-technology image, the total absence of the tactile element (you can't touch the merchandise in the kiosk), the costs of development, and the mostly overstated claim that kiosks are "too inhuman."

Some industry observers say that the introduction of electronic retailing on a mass scale will go the way of automatic teller machines—a slow, if not skeptical acceptance followed by mass usage once people got used to them. It is fair to say that electronic retailing will also have its snafus, because it combines the imprecise product of software engineering and generally reliable but emerging technologies like touchscreen and CD players. But, based on the initial response to the introduction of electronic retailing by major retail chains like Sears, Penney's, and Dayton Hudson, the retailing industry is undeniably enthusiastic and willing to explore interactive video to its fullest possible extent. Indeed, interactive video has been embraced by U.S. companies to a much greater extent than has any other sector of videotex.

Early Trials

The major retailers exploring interactive video are entering the market cautiously. Compared to nonelectronic displays, the costs of interactive video are much higher, require more careful development, and are more difficult to evaluate in retailing environments that have previously had no interactive displays. Two of the early entrants into interactive retailing—Comp-U-Card International and CompuSave—conducted limited tests and pulled their kiosks out of stores to re-evaluate their marketing strategies. Industry analysts said the pullbacks were due to electronic catalog offerings that were not related to the environments in which they were placed. For example, CompuSave's terminals were placed in supermarkets, but they displayed a wide variety of consumer goods that could not be found in that environment. People were not used to shopping for TVs and VCRs on a machine placed in a supermarket, some analysts suggested.

A more direct marketing strategy is being adopted by E & B Marine of Edison, New Jersey, which is the first client of R.R. Donnelly's Electronistore Services. E & B has placed seven Electronistore kiosks in its marine supply stores. The terminals feature boating gear such as radios, anchors, and other accessories. Other terminals will eventually be placed with high-volume boat dealers who would not stock boating accessories. E & B executives say that, if their trial is successful, they will install 400 terminals within three years.

Much of interactive retailing's success or failure will depend upon the marketer's ability to create new, "mini" buying environments through combinations of product with presentation. There seems to be little question as to the efficacy of video as a selling medium. It has all the power of television and niche marketing. Its ability to streamline and affect customer buying patterns will be undisputed in the near future.

Getting Started in Interactive Merchandising

A highly advisable way to begin a trial in electronic retailing is to select a range of products that could move faster if presented in a kiosk. Because selectivity is really controlled by the retailer through the choice of products displayed in the kiosk, using electronic retailing against a "control" situation would be a good experiment. A control involves a similar selling situation in which a kiosk would not be involved. Such a trial situation would provide a comparison of the two methods of selling a range of products.

Once the product range is determined, choice of an electronic retailing product depends upon how the material is to be presented. Will the kiosk display still images or moving images, use sound or allow the user to order from the kiosk? To arrive at a workable strategy, two distinctions must first be made:

- Will the kiosk be dedicated to a strictly informational display?
- Will the kiosk also be used to process transactions through a built-in credit card reader?

Although development costs vary widely depending upon the scope of a project, the bulk of the cost of developing your electronic retailing program will be consumed in software development. This means that frames must be created, video images recorded, a database organized, and the entire package coordinated with the touchscreen commands and optional audio track (actually the simplest part since CDs record image and sound on the same disk).

Costs

An electronic retailing project can be developed for anywhere from $50,000 to more than $300,000. The bulk of these costs represents software development. Costs of software development—usually priced separately because it is linked to the scope of the information to be stored—can run into six figures. But, once an electronic retailing program is finished, it is easily updated and duplicated for about fifteen percent of the initial development cost, industry experts say. The kiosks themselves, usually packaged with all the necessary hardware provided by a handful of vendors, cost from $10,000 to $20,000 each.

Unfortunately, there is no rule of thumb as to what an electronic retailing project should cost. It is a nascent industry dealing with hundreds of trial projects at this point in time. Industry executives claim that single machines could take in from $60,00 to $100,000 annually. The accounting firm of Touche Ross, in a widely cited report, estimated that a kiosk could generate $100,000 in sales a year by 1990. That's based on an average of five sales a day at $60 per transaction.

As far as development costs go, it's difficult to determine what a bargain is or what's too expensive. Any cost/benefit analysis has to be based on expected performance since there are no set formulas to predict the amount that kiosks should yield in sales volume per year.

The Major Vendors

Choosing a vendor is a matter of determining which firm can provide all the necessary services to build an effective electronic retailing. A full-service vendor can provide both software and hardware. Although the hardware is generally easier to obtain than the software, the combination of both capabilities in a vendor is considered an asset. Track record is also important. See a functioning kiosk in a store before you decide on a vendor. If you can't understand how the kiosk works and you can't see it selling in another store, chances are that you won't be able to make it work in your retail setting. Another good way of checking the track record of a vendor is to ask other retailers about the service they have received and the amount they paid for it. Note that the most expensive component of your electronic retailing strategy could be software development. Some other suggestions to consider before you approach a vendor:

- Starting small is better than starting big. Start with a limited range of products.
- Have some idea of how you want your products presented. Will computer graphics in NAPLPS do? (NAPLPS stands for North American Presentation Level Protocol Standard.) Or do you require full-motion video, which can be more expensive depending upon your presentation?
- Make a sales goal for the kiosks as if they were salesmen, but make conservative estimates. They are new and untried. You can construct payback scenarios based on these projections.
- What kind of software do you need? In addition to the software that will run your presentation, you might require usage tracking, order entry, and telecommunications. The last two are needed for transactional kiosks. A good vendor can supply and program this software.

The companies profiled in the following section represent the most active vendors in electronic retailing. Although new companies are starting up every month, these firms have established themselves early on as fairly significant participants in the marketplace. As with the other firms cited in this book, these company overviews do not attempt to make any technical or evaluative claims about the companies' products or services. These profiles are designed to acquaint you with the range of services and products available. The addresses and telephone numbers of the companies are available in Appendix C.

ByVideo, Inc. ByVideo has been one of the most visible companies in electronic retailing. It is a full-service firm that offers hardware, software, networking, and video services.

In addition to kiosks for Marshall Fields, ByVideo has sold its UniPort system to the Florsheim Shoe Co., which has installed kiosks in Thayer McNeil stores and shopping malls. ByVideo also designed and built kiosks for Avon Products, which sells its products in office buildings and shopping malls.

Cableshare Cableshare is primarily a software development house that also offers time-sharing capabilities. It has developed projects for the Bank of Montreal, Canada Trust, and Simpsons and Younkers department stores.

This Canadian company, thirty-six percent owned by J.C. Penney, is also known for its involvement in the software in R.R. Donnelly's Electronistore system. Cableshare also has associations with Digital Equipment, Ford, GTE, Videolog, and American Express. Additionally, it should be noted that Cableshare was one of the early entrants into videotex with its Picture Painter NAPLPS frame-creation terminal, which is used extensively in the industry.

Digital Techniques A software and hardware development company with diverse interests, Digital Techniques is marketing and supporting its Touchcom interactive video system. The system can be designed to perform retailing, banking, and training applications.

The company has developed kiosks for the Eyeworks retail chain, which uses the devices to aid customers in selecting from among more than 4,000 frame styles of eyeglasses. Digital has also designed an instructional delivery system for Raytheon, which has a marketing agreement with the company. In addition to its other products, Digital sells a workstation that can produce a customized interactive video product.

Electronistore R.R. Donnelly's Electronistore offers both software and hardware development and full client support. It is marketing its free-standing electronic retailing kiosk that combines touchscreen and transactional capabilities.

Electronistore's first client—E & B Marine of Edison, New Jersey—is using the kiosks to sell marine products in its retail locations and at trade shows.

Interac Corp. Interac has had extensive experience in developing interactive video systems for both public access and corporate use. Its central product is called ASCIT (Automated System for Consumer Information and Training).

A full-service company, Interac's clients are Monsanto, General Electric, Sony, AT&T, and the Cowles Media Company. For example, Monsanto has been testing Interac kiosks to market carpet samples in J.C. Penney stores. At this writing, Interac was also testing products for General Electric and the J. Paul Getty Museum. An Interac system was also featured at Disney's Epcot Center.

Interactive Training Systems, Inc. ITS develops and markets systems for merchandising and banking. This full-service firm also makes systems for corporate training.

To date, the largest client of ITS is Sears, which has been testing ITS kiosks in its stores to market window coverings (draperies and curtains) and the Sears Financial Network.

ELECTRONIC BANKING FOR PERSONAL COMPUTERS

Online database/videotex technology also enables personal computer users to access their personal or business bank accounts at home or in the office. Although this is the most nascent of the advanced applications, it holds some promise for integrating the computer with banking functions.

Despite the capabilities of "telebanking," most of the banking packages available for business and personal computer users are expensive (costlier than going to the bank yourself) and limited. Of the vendors worth exploring (see Appendix C), a trial period might be in order for Chase Manhattan's Spectrum, Chemical Bank's Pronto, and similar services from Citicorp, Manufacturers Hanover, and Bank of America.

Eventually, fully integrated electronic banking services will allow you to take your personal or business banking data and insert it into any spreadsheet, database, or accounting management program. Some current services allow you to use your banking service with a spreadsheet. Most of the services, however, are somewhat limited and are much more useful for their ability to transfer funds. These services should become more useful as the online services become more popular with corporate financial departments.

Banking via videotex, video banking, or telebanking is one of the most promising business applications of videotex that had already well established itself as a consumer videotex product. Banks offering the services had invested more than $500 million in twenty-three pilots and twenty-eight services. Unfortunately, the cost efficiency of telebanking—based on the current electronic banking services on the market—may not be one of its prime attributes.

Telebanking is generally more expensive than conventional banking because there may be additional charges associated with telecommunications, online connect time, or just the privilege of using the banking service electronically. And, in many cases, telebanking provides a poor example of efficiency since, in many cases, going directly to the bank may process your transaction faster. Other problems include the need for businesses to make the investment in personal computers and modems in order to use the services as well as lack of universal standards and, therefore, compatibility.

Although most popular personal computers can access telebanking services, a business must perform its transactions with one bank exclusively on each of the services. For example, you cannot use Citibank's service to access your account at Chase and vice versa. It may also be difficult to perform cash flow analysis using one of the current banking programs or even print out necessary information from the banking service because the software might not work. Having more than two accounts would aid small businesses in telebanking by giving them more flexibility.

The benefits of telebanking arise from the ability to use a personal computer to manage any number of financial transactions. Personal computers, by virtue of their ability to run money management programs, can show you in a short period of time a record of expenditures and calculate any number of variations with the figures you can choose to input.

Software Compatibility

Programs like Moneylink and Dollars and Sense are designed to work with some of the larger telebanking systems to allow you to do financial planning and conduct transactions with a bank. For example, you can create a list of funds transfers and payments, and Moneylink will, at your command, send those instructions directly to the bank's computer. Although the programs available for the telebanking services are not as sophisticated as many spreadsheet programs, they allow for more efficient display, storage, and manipulation of your financial data. It also should be noted those programs are geared for personal financial management, not business.

In addition, telebanking may streamline bookkeeping and cash management practices. Debits and credits are registered and stored electronically, and it is a simple matter to see if certain bills have been paid and checks have cleared. In this respect, having a direct connection with a bank's computer is far more efficient than dealing with account officers and tellers or trying to unravel a payment problem over the phone. Also, the telebanking services provide for twenty-four-hour interaction with bank computers. That may, however, be a moot point since many transactions might not be processed until a day after you send them to the bank computer.

For small businesses, the time savings could be sizable for a system that permits instantaneous transactions, funds transfers, and easy access to other customer services like lines of credit. Unfortunately, as of this writing, no service offers these features.

Several consumer services offer a selected array of banking services that utilize a personal computer both as a terminal and accounting system. At the end of 1985, there were nearly 60,000 individual users of telebanking services. Since there were only two services that provided separate services for businesses, it was difficult to tell if businesses were using the home services. Telebanking has been extremely successful in France, where the Teletel service is capable of delivering those services to 1.4 million French homes. But that's because the French government invested several billion francs in their own national videotex system. No such system exists in the U.S.

Of the total number of telebanking users, it is estimated that less than 4,000 were using these services for business. There is one important distinction that should be made about telebanking services for personal computers. It has yet to reach the point where it can link electronic payments to purchase orders, take specific commands from a spreadsheet program, and do large-scale funds transfers. There are much larger systems that are able to handle high-volume funds transfers, but the services described in this chapter are generally to be used for small-scale applications on personal computers for small businesses of not more than 100 employees.

Telebanking Technology

Some telebanking systems are based on systems that employ *electronic funds transfer* (EFT). This medium of exchange is the virtually paperless process of moving funds from one computer system to another. The only paper or money involved comes in the form of a confirmation notice. EFT is a technology that has been around for several years and is used by all the major banks. Customers of these banks are linked to the EFT systems for accounts payable, receivable, and payroll. Several "money center" or large regional or international banks even provide a complete range of data-processing services that revolve around cash management and EFT.

Telebanking utilizes EFT on a much smaller scale than the larger, commercial EFT systems. The automatic teller machines (ATMs) that have become extremely popular in recent years also use EFT. However, unlike ATMs, electronic banking systems available to personal computer users will not dispense hard currency, nor are they expected to do so in the near future.

If a system does not use EFT to move messages or funds electronically, it will use a method called *batch-mode processing*. Batch mode simply stores all the messages it receives over the period of one day, bundles them up, and passes them on to a bank computer all at once—usually late at night. This way, when a message or request for a fund transfer is sent through a service using batch mode, it will not be registered until the next day. Compared to EFT, batch mode is much slower. EFT is instantaneous, whereas it may be faster to process a transaction by walking into a bank instead of using a service that uses batch-mode processing—a distinct disadvantage if immediate funds transfer is indicated.

Electronic banking does, however, streamline the whole process of transactions ordinarily performed by a human teller. Although electronic banking is limited to the capabilities of a keyboard and computer, it can:

- Pay bills electronically to a predesignated list of payees, sending funds via the system to the companies you want to receive payment for your bills.
- Transfer funds to or from separate accounts.

- Provide account balance information twenty-four hours a day.
- Integrate with personal finance software.
- Provide gateways to business information services like Dow Jones News Retrieval.
- Obtain information on other banking services.
- Open new accounts.
- Obtain information on credit card accounts.
- Send E-mail to the bank and other users.
- Check status of check clearing.

Major Vendors

Although there are more regional banks than money center banks involved in telebanking, the few money center banks that offer telebanking services are the goliaths of the banking industry. These banks seeded their telebanking services in order to attract more affluent retail banking customers who owned personal computers and to trim some of their own operating costs on the retail side. Telebanking is, in fact, more an outgrowth of the banks' attempt to cut costs through innovations like the twenty-four-hour electronic teller machines (and not having to pay a salary for a human teller) than it is a genuine commitment to videotex per se. Bank holding companies like Citicorp and Bank of America have made long-term commitments to add as many electronic services as possible in an effort to combat soaring operating costs.

Telebanking is a true videotex application because it combines the strengths of a computer, data communications, and software that makes it accessible to nearly any user. Unlike the large-scale EFT systems used by Fortune 500 companies and the banks themselves, most telebanking systems are simple. The software that runs telebanking services generates a handful of menus that offer the user a choice of options. Once the user has made a choice, the software will either store it or send a message to its "host" banking computer via a modem and telephone line. Because telecommunications charges are cheapest for local calls, most telebanking services cater to customers in a given metropolitan area or state.

The majority of the key money center bank telebanking services are based in New York—coincidentally where the five largest banks in the country (except for Bank of America) have their headquarters. New York is not only the most competitive market for telebanking, it's an important testing ground for telebanking nationwide. The New York area also has a relatively high concentration of personal computer users who might be willing to subscribe to the services. Among the leaders in the Big Apple are Citibank's Direct Access; Chase Manhattan Bank's Spectrum; Manufacturers Hanover's Excel; and Chemical Bank's Pronto, which has since been absorbed into Covidea, the entity that began the development and marketing of telebanking services on a large scale in mid-1985.

COVIDEA

Covidea's Target Service

Covidea is a consortium that includes Chemical Bank, AT&T, Time, and, when approval is formally granted by the U.S. Comptroller of the Currency, Bank of America (BOA). Although BOA had not received approval as of this writing, it has been participating in Covidea development. Both Chemical Bank and BOA bring their own home banking services into Covidea, which will be marketing them under the Covidea umbrella. AT&T is expected to contribute its expertise in the computer terminal business. The AT&T 1300 terminal, a small portable terminal (not a fully operational personal computer) will be marketed by Covidea for "under $100" so that Covidea users can directly access the service from home. Time, whose role was not clearly defined at the early-1986 start of service, was expected to be an information provider.

Costs

The combination of Chemical Bank's Pronto and BOA's Hometeller service totals more than 40,000 subscribers. When BOA receives formal federal approval, it too will be marketed by Covidea as a Covidea product. Until then, it will be a separate service, offered at $8 a month. In the meantime, the core product for Covidea will be Pronto, which has nearly 23,000 subscribers and charges $12 a month.

Basic pricing for the Business Banker service is $30/month for two checking accounts, but does not include telecommunications charges, basic business account charges, or the added charges that may be incurred in using its online stock quotation or trading service.

Covidea is more than just a telebanking service, since it plans to offer a discount brokerage and stock quotation service. The firm will also offer "incentives" to regional banks to join the service as Covidea franchisees. As of this writing, though, only one bank had done so.

Covidea's Business Banking Service

The main business service offered through Covidea is Pronto's Business Banker, which was in pilot phase at this writing. It is essentially the same service as Pronto, only equipped with what Covidea calls "customized control," which allows only certain personnel with access codes into specified accounts. Gaining access to the system requires a personal identification code and two other levels of identification.

A separate group of bankers within Chemical handles Business Banker customers. That gives Business Banker customers access (through E-mail) to telebanking and a wide range of services, including cash management, trusts, and payroll management—although those services may not be directly available through Business Banker. Among the separate features available on Business Banker are:

- Funds transfer in batch mode.
- Balance information on business checking, revolving credit line, savings, and money market accounts.
- Electronic statements listing debits and credits and allowing hard-copy printouts, provided you have a printer.
- Online checkbook register showing when checks clear and allowing checks to be called up by number. (A feature called "electronic reconciliation worksheet" will compute a balance.)
- Rate information.
- Electronic mail with twenty-four-hour messaging to account officers.
- Bill paying by transfer of funds to predesignated accounts.

The Business Banker service is also being designed to include the ability to interface with Lotus 1-2-3 software and Microsoft Multiplan, although, at this writing, no specific date for the introduction of that product was available.

BOA's service is tailored for consumers and offers some useful interfaces with Moneylink—a $50 program that connects a personal finance software package called Dollars and Sense (from $100 to $180) to BOA. This service, however unsuitable for small businesses, is worth a look if for no other reason than to sample the possibilities of telebanking.

CHASE MANHATTAN BANK

Chase was one of the first of the big banks to enter telebanking. It began to experiment with the concept in 1981—back when videotex was just a gleam in a few corporations' eyes. Spectrum emerged in 1984 and, according to Chase, has attracted more users than anticipated.

Spectrum is a consumer service that has separate levels

of features that may prove versatile for small businesses. One of those levels, Spectrum for Business, offers:

- Funds transfer, assigning authorized users a specific dollar-per-transaction limit.
- Bill payment including records of the transaction.
- Account balances within ninety days of past activity.
- Electronic checkbook to keep track of all transactions and enable stop payments.
- Spending tracker to keep a record of all disbursements.
- Money transfer by wire.
- Commercial Loan Inquiry.
- Investment services that allow users to access stock quotations, place buy and sell orders via Chase's Rose and Co. discount brokerage, and access online stock market letters, Standard and Poor's corporate research, and a financial planning service.
- Electronic mail to Spectrum customer service.
- Chase products and rate guide.

Costs

Basic pricing for Spectrum is $5 a month. Options such as the stock quotation/broker service are an additional $5 a month. The investment information ranges from $4 to $5 a month. Portfolio management is available for $6 a month. The service is available through an 800 number. The business service is available for $50 a month.

CITIBANK

Citibank's Direct Access also offers an interface to Moneylink and Dollars and Sense. This relationship will enable users to "download" (send information from the user's terminal to another computer) monthly statements to Citibank.

Although Direct Access has no counterpart for small

business, Citibank officials say they are developing a small business service. No introduction date was available at this writing.

Direct Access may be useful to business users since it has many of the features of the other services on the market, such as twenty-four-hour funds transfer, bill payment, account information, and electronic mail. A worthwhile option available to Direct Access users is a free password to Dow Jones News Retrieval (DJNR), a service which carries *Wall Street Journal* stories, Dow Jones News-wire reports, and financial market quotations, and has powerful business research capabilities. Normally, the DJNR password would cost $75. Citibank also provides $25 in free DJNR usage. After the free time is used up, Citibank will bill its customers at DJNR connect time rates, some of which go up to $60 an hour.

Another useful feature on Direct Access is the capability to download information into a spreadsheet program like Lotus 1-2-3, PFS:Plan, Dollars and Sense, and Symphony. In effect, information from the telebanking service can be shifted and stored in the spreadsheet programs for further manipulation. It should also be noted that funds transfers are processed in batch mode.

Costs

Pricing for the service is $10 a month, with the first two months free on a trial basis. Unfortunately, the service can be (economically) used only in the New York area.

MANUFACTURERS HANOVER TRUST (MHT)

"Manny Hanny," as MHT is affectionately known in the banking industry, launched its Excel service in late 1984. The consumer service focuses on personal financial management through MHT's marketing of Electronic Arts' Financial Cookbook financial management program. Standard features include bill payment to ninety-nine payees, funds transfers, balance information, and electronic mail. As of this writing, MHT had made no announcement about a separate service for businesses, as it was in a pilot-testing phase. In conjunction with Excel, the Philadelphia National Bank was also piloting a business telebanking service.

Costs

Pricing for the consumer service is available on a $100-a-year basis or $12 a month.

OTHER TELEBANKING VENDORS

Compuserve is home not only to a good selection of business videotex services but to four separate telebanking services that are offered by regional banks and operated by Video Financial Services, a Dallas-based telebanking firm. The consumer services are available through Compuserve's network, so you must be a Compuserve subscriber to access them in addition to having accounts at the banks. The banks involved are NCNB, Charlotte, North Carolina; Southeast Bank, Miami; Bank One, Columbus, Ohio; NCR Universal Credit Union and PSFS, Philadelphia. Several other services were offered through the defunct Gateway and Viewtron consumer videotex services, but have since re-evaluated their telebanking operations.

These services are similar to one another in that they offer bill payment, account balances, funds transfer, and electronic mail to the banks. The services tend to be more expensive than those offered by the New York banks because they require payment of Compuserve connect time charges (ranging from $6 to $16 an hour), telecommunications charges, and bank charges. As of this writing, these services were designed primarily for consumers, but they may also serve as good introductions to businesses served by those regional banks that want to survey telebanking.

One business banking service that uses Compuserve's

network but does not require subscribers to be Compuserve subscribers, is Shawmut Bank's (Boston) Business Arrive, which is available for $35 a month per account. The service was largely under development at this writing but did offer bill paying, funds transfer, account balance checks, and a tax tip service.

REGIONAL TELEBANKING SERVICES

Several regional banks are either offering, developing, or considering development projects involving telebanking. Some of the more visible services have been launched by Madison National Bank, Washington, D.C.; Penn Security and Trust, Scranton, PA; Empire of America, Buffalo, NY; and the National Bank of Detroit. Of these banks, Madison National has been most active in developing services for the business arena.

THE FUTURE OF TELEBANKING

Successful telebanking systems will be fully able to employ all the benefits of electronic funds transfer to make cash management more efficient for businesses. In order for telebanking to become cost efficient, it must be offered at rates comparable to or lower than those of current business banking services. Telebanking for small businesses can be an effective extension of banking services that will integrate a host of bookkeeping and cash management software with telebanking services. Regional banks, though limited by capital development–funding constraints, will be likely to follow the leads of the New York banks and Covidea.

Telebanking by itself will probably not be the cause of the wide dissemination of videotex. Coupled with information services, electronic mail, database access and retrieval, closed user-group capabilities, and electronic publishing, telebanking is but one component of videotex that could make financial management for businesses more efficient.

Regional banks will be able to enter the telebanking arena by making licensing agreements with Covidea or by buying their own hardware through vendors such as Digital or Shuttle. Telebanking systems can be installed with relatively cost-effective minicomputers and existing telephone networks.

Faced with increasingly larger marketing and service costs, many regional banks might perceive telebanking as a way of extending services and cutting costs by eliminating the additional expenses of direct service through tellers and account and loan officers. For the banks, telebanking may represent an economical way of dispensing information like account balances, loan programs, lines of credit, and account descriptions. Combined with electronic mail capabilities, banks may be able to extend funds transfer and twenty-four-hour access to account information to a market of small- and medium-sized businesses that would normally have to wait for the bank to open to obtain services.

However, to reach small businesses, only a high degree of service and direct, real-time access to account information, funds transfer, and cash management software will make telebanking feasible on a large scale. Businesses also need to be able to monitor funds in a large number of accounts. As the services are priced as this goes to press, telebanking is more expensive than conventional banking and offers considerably less in the way of service. The convenience factor may not be worth the extra cost. There is also a problem with software compatibility.

In summary, telebanking services for businesses will need to offer sophisticated software that will allow multiple retrieval and storage of account information and perform tasks like cash flow analysis. At this writing, the only software programs compatible with telebanking services are oriented to the home user. One factor definitely favoring telebanking for business, though, is falling prices for business-oriented computers like the IBM PC and the high number of personal computers already in use in the business environment. Telebanking does have a place in the business environment because of its natural relationship to office and financial automation once the technology itself matures.

And, as the technology becomes more prevalent, refined, and accepted on a large scale, telebanking for business could become a welcome fixture in a business's automated financial management scheme.

THE FUTURE

Infocentric offices of the future will consolidate all the tasks that were previously done by separate systems. There will be one system for word processing, telex, copying, printing, personal and mainframe computing, E-mail, and database searching. In short, one system will serve all the organization's information needs.

Artificial intelligence will also play a large part in infocentric offices. Instead of accessing hundreds of databases with several phone calls, you will be able to talk to a device that will do the research for you. This "expert" system will also be able to question you to refine your search. According to this scenario, getting specialized business information will be easier than using a vending machine.

No matter what technology is developed to make computing and information access more efficient, databases will still be used to store information. Information consumers who know where to find information and how to use that information will always benefit from their skills. In an infocentric organization, it's not the information that's so critical, it's the transformation of the information into something more powerful—knowledge.

APPENDIX A
ANNOTATED BIBLIOGRAPHY

Cuadra Associates, Inc., *Directory of Online Databases,* Santa Monica, CA: Cuadra Associates, Inc. (1985). One of the most comprehensive guides to more than 3,000 databases and database producers. Indispensable to the newcomer and expert alike.

Mike Edelhart and Owen Davies, *The Omni Online Database Directory,* New York: Omni Publications International Ltd. (1984). Although not as complete as the Cuadra directory, an excellent resource, especially for novices and researchers.

Elizabeth Ferrarini, *Infomania,* Boston: Houghton Mifflin Co. (1985). An extensive, easy-to-use guide that combines humor with practical advice.

Alfred Glossbrenner, *The Complete Handbook of Personal Computer Communications,* New York: St. Martin's Press (1986). Explains computers, databases, and communications in friendly prose. For novice or intermediate computer users.

Ryan Hoover, *Executive's Guide to Online Information Services,* White Plains, New York: Knowledge Industry Publications, Inc. (1984). A practical how-to guide chock-full of examples of online database applications.

Doran Howitt and Marvin Weinberger, *Databasics Your Guide to Business Information,* New York: Garland Publishing (1986). One of the most popular and useful volumes on everything concerning business databases, brokers, software, and hardware. Also explains searching and has valuable coupons for products and services.

Matthew Lesko, *The Computer Data and Database Source Book,* New York: Avon Books (1986). A thorough listing of nearly every public and private database available. The section on government databases and information sources is especially useful.

APPENDIX B

INFORMATION BROKERS

FIND/SVP
500 5th Ave.
New York, NY 10110
Telephone: (212) 354-2424
Telex: 148358

This broker/research service will search all major databases, 900 journals, and 15,000 subject files. Although FIND/SVP prefers to work on a retainer basis, it is possible to order individual market research reports on a number of subjects and industries. The average search time turnaround is twenty-four to forty-eight hours. Custom research is available. Two services called Competitive and Business Intelligence Alerts will scan online databases for specific information.

Information on Demand
P.O. Box 1370
Berkeley, CA 94701
Telephone: (415) 644-4500; (800) 227-0750
Telex: 6501347171
Also available through BRS, ORBIT, Dialorder, ONTYME, or Science Net.

Owned by Pergamon International, the respected publisher and database vendor, IOD searches all major databases and has access to a number of important academic libraries. IOD will also locate, acquire, or photocopy articles, documents, catalogs, annual reports, competitors' brochures, foreign articles, theses, patents, and technical literature. Translation, telephone interviews, and secondary market research are also available. A true full-service broker.

> Information Store, Inc.
> 140 Second St.
> San Francisco, CA 94105
> Telephone: (415) 543-4636
> Cable: INFOSTORE

This broker does nearly everything in the way of database searching, document delivery, and specialized research. The company says it specializes in business, marketing, and law. Prepayment or retainer accounts are preferred with discounts of up to twenty-five percent available to regular users.

> INFO/DOC
> P.O. Box 17109, Dulles Airport
> Washington, DC 20041
> Telephone: (800) 336-0800

An information retrieval and document delivery service, INFO/DOC is a broker that specializes in government information. The service is an authorized distributor for National Technical Information Service and Government Printing Office products and publications. A rush service is available. Other services focusing on medical research and reference and census data are also offered.

> Information USA
> 4701 Willard Ave., Suite 1707
> Chevy Chase, MD 20815
> Telephone: (301) 657-1200

Also available through Compuserve, Information USA will put you in touch with an expert in specific areas. Although not a full-service information broker, Information USA specializes in government information and expertise.

> Pergamon ORBIT Infoline, Inc.
> 1340 Old Chain Bridge Rd.
> McLean, VA 22101
> Telephone: (703) 442-0900; (800) 336-7575
> Telex: 90-1811

This company specializes in technical, trademark, and patent databases. You can use their online system to search, or they can search for you.

> Research One
> P.O. Box 795 549, Dept. 309
> Dallas, TX 75379
> Telephone: (214) 233-1477; (800) 225-0227 (code 99 3068)

Specializing in rush service, Research One also performs current awareness programs and analysis of retrieved data. They will search Dialog, BRS, Pergamon ORBIT Infoline, and Datasolve.

> UMI Article Clearinghouse
> 300 N. Zeeb Rd.
> Ann Arbor, MI 48106
> Telephone: (313) 761-4700; (800) 732-0616
> Also available through ONTYME and Dialcom.

This Bell & Howell unit, the distribution arm of University Microfilm International, is primarily in the business of delivering articles from more than 8,000 publications. The service generally has a forty-eight-hour turnaround and provides a twenty-four-hour service for an additional $5. The pricing is advantageous for volume ordering. Dissertations and books are also available.

APPENDIX C
VENDORS, SERVICES, AND TRADE GROUPS

The following is a list of vendors and organizations that specialize in private databases, electronic mail, electronic banking, interactive retailing, and videotex services.

VENDORS

ADP Autonet
175 Jackson Plaza
Ann Arbor, MI 48106
Telephone: (313) 769-6800

ADP produces a service called Automail that incorporates electronic mail, bulletin boards, a corporate directory, and courier service.

BRS Information Technologies
1200 Route 7
Latham, NY 12110
Telephone: (800) 345-4277; (518) 783-1161

BRS offers private database development services and three online-database services in BRS/Search, BRS/After Dark, and BRS/BRKTHRU.

ByVideo
225 Humboldt Ct.
Sunnyvale, CA 94089
Telephone: (408) 747-1101

ByVideo manufactures interactive video shopping terminals and software. The company also provides support to clients in the production of the presentation material.

Cableshare
P.O. Box 5880
20 Enterprise Drive
London, Ontario, Canada N6A 4L6
Telephone: (519) 686-2900

Cableshare supplies videotex software, hardware, and support. Its electronic marketing division developed the Touch N' Shop retailing system.

Compuserve
5000 Arlington Centre Blvd.
P.O. Box 20212
Columbus, OH 43220
Telephone: (614) 457-8600

This company produces and offers support for consumer and business videotex services, private databases, and an electronic mail service. Its Interchange service is geared to business.

Covidea/Target
300 Jericho Quadrangle
Jericho, NY 11753
Telephone: (516) 937-7000

A joint venture of AT&T, Chemical Bank, Time, and Bank of America that is offering a consumer/business electronic banking service.

VENDORS, SERVICES, AND TRADE GROUPS   189

Delphi (General Videotex Corp.)
3 Blackstone St.
Cambridge, MA 02139
Telephone: (800) 544-4005; (617) 491-3393

General Videotex's Delphi is a videotex service/online utility. It also offers Grouplink, a private database service, and other business and consumer communications and database services.

Dialcom
6120 Executive Blvd.
Rockville, MD 20852
Telephone: (301) 881-9020

Dialcom is an online-database vendor and provider of electronic mail, conferencing, bulletin boards, and private databases.

Digital Equipment Corp. (DEC)
Merrimack, NH 03054-0430
Telephone: (603) 884-5111

Digital offers extensive videotex hardware and software packages, office automation, CD-ROM, voice synthesis, and minicomputing systems.

Digital Techniques
10 'B' Street
Burlington, MA 01803
Telephone: (617) 273-3495

This company markets and supports its Touchcom system for electronic retailing and banking applications. Hardware and software for interactive video are also available.

Direct Access
Citibank, N.A.
P.O. Box 5126, Grand Central Station
New York, NY 10163-5126
Telephone: (800) 248-4472

This Citibank-operated home electronic banking service is available to personal computer owners.

Electronistore
2122 York Rd., Suite 360
Oak Brook, IL 60521
Telephone: (312) 574-4900

A subsidiary of the publishing giant R.R. Donnelly & Sons, Electronistore markets an electronic retailing system that combines videodisk, stereo, and transactional functions.

EXCEL
Manufacturers Hanover Trust Co.
P.O. Box 2724, Grand Central Station
New York, NY 10163
Telephone: (800) 643-9325; (212) 286-6000

Excel is a twenty-four-hour electronic banking and money management service available to personal computer users.

Foursquare Software
122 N. Main St.
Hendersonville, NC 28739
Telephone: (704) 692-2565

A software developer that supports its own videotex system, specializing in order entry and inventory control.

General Electric Corp.
Information Services Co.
401 N. Washington St.
Rockville, MD 20850
Telephone: (301) 251-6510

VENDORS, SERVICES, AND TRADE GROUPS 191

GE markets several communication and time-sharing computer services such as Quick-Comm (electronic mail), GEnie (consumer videotex), and Mark III.

> GTE Telenet
> 12490 Sunrise Valley Dr.
> Reston, VA 22096
> Telephone: (800) TELENET

Through its Telenet division, GTE offers telecommunications packet-switching network services and its Telemail electronic mail service.

> Honeywell Infonow
> Honeywell Information Systems
> 4849 N. Scott St.
> Schiller Park, IL 60176
> Telephone: (312) 671-1800

Infonow is Honeywell's business videotex system. Honeywell markets hardware, software, support, and training for the system.

> Infomart
> 164 Merton St.
> Toronto, Ontario, Canada M4S 3A8
> Telephone: (416) 489-6640

The company supplies and produces videotex hardware and software including Teleguide and Grassroots. It also designs videotex services.

> Interac
> 12555 W. Jefferson Blvd., Suite 175
> Los Angeles, CA 90066
> Telephone: (213) 301-7640

Interac designs interactive video systems and provides hardware and software support. It markets its ASCIT videodisk system.

Interactive Training Systems
9 Oak Park Dr.
Bedford, MA 01730
Telephone: (800) 227-1127; (617) 271-0500

ITS is a designer of interactive video systems for corporate training, banking, and electronic retailing. It also supports and markets hardware and software for the systems.

Security Pacific National Bank
P.O. Box 7150
Brea, CA 92622-7150
Telephone: (714) 961-2833

This bank offers an electronic banking service called ReadyAccess PC Banking for consumers and a business banking service called PC Business Banking.

Shuttle
2565 152nd Ave. NE
Redmond, WA 98052
Telephone: (206) 882-3447

Shuttle manufactures videotex systems including its Scratch Pad system, which can be accessed by personal computers.

The Source
1616 Anderson Rd.
McLean, VA 22102
Telephone: (703) 734-7500

An online utility, The Source offers electronic mail, teleconferencing, private business databases, special interest groups, and bulletin boards.

Spectrum
The Chase Manhattan Bank, N.A.

VENDORS, SERVICES, AND TRADE GROUPS 193

P.O. Box 5144
New Hyde Park, NY 11042
Telephone: (800) 522-7766; (212) 223-7794

Chase offers consumer and business banking services that are available to personal computer users. Service can also access the Rose discount brokerage program.

Tandy/Radio Shack
Videotex Department
1400 One Tandy Center
Fort Worth, TX 76102
Telephone: (817) 390-2642

Radio Shack markets and supports its VIS videotex system, which runs on a Tandy 6000 computer. Related hardware and software packages are sold through Radio Shack retail outlets.

Trintex
445 Hamilton Ave.
White Plains, NY 10601
Telephone: (914) 993-8000

This joint venture of IBM and Sears is expected to launch a videotex service in 1988 that will cater to consumers using personal computers.

Videolog
50 Washington St.
Norwalk, CT 06854
Telephone: (800) VIDEOLOG; (203) 838-5100

A videotex system operator that owns and operates the system by the same name. Videolog is an online catalog of electronic components that specializes in semiconductors.

Western Union
1 Lake St.

Upper Saddle River, NJ 07458
Telephone: (800) 527-5184

Through its EasyLink service, Western Union provides electronic mail, telex, news, document delivery, online databases, and a host of other services.

SOURCES FOR MORE INFORMATION

American Society for Information Science
1424 16th St., NW, Suite 404
Washington, DC 20036
Telephone: (202) 462-1000

A professional society for information specialists such as information brokers and librarians. ASIS publishes a newsletter and directory of information companies and professionals.

Arlen Communications, Inc.
P.O. Box 40871
Washington, DC 20016
Telephone: (301) 656-7940

The publisher of the authoritative newsletter *International Videotex and Teletext News* and the *Videotex Directory*.

Electronic Mail Association
1919 Pennsylvania Ave., NW, Suite 300
Washington, DC 20006
Telephone: (202) 293-7808

This trade group can handle inquiries on the industry, monitor relevant legislation, and promote research.

Information Industry Association
555 N. New Jersey Ave., NW, Suite 800
Washington, DC 20001
Telephone: (202) 639-8262

The IIA is the primary organization and lobby supporting the top 2,000 companies in the information industry. Its membership includes banks, computer firms, consultants, online-database vendors, and related corporations in information processing, CD-ROM, electronic publishing, videotex, and teletext. The IIA also sponsors conferences and publishes newsletters and directories. It is a good source for information on the industry, its members, and consultants. Regional IIA chapters meet on a regular basis.

>   Institute for the Future
>   2740 Sand Hill Road
>   Menlo Park, CA 94025-7097
>   Telephone: (415) 854-6322

The institute researches and issues reports on videotex, teleconferencing, and teletext.

>   International Resource Development, Inc.
>   6 Prowitt St.
>   Norwalk, CT 06855
>   Telephone: (203) 866-6914

This firm publishes two newsletters on electronic mail and videotex—*EMMS* and *Videoprint*. It also publishes a wealth of research on those industries.

>   Knowledge Industry Publications, Inc.
>   701 Westchester Ave.
>   White Plains, NY 10604
>   Telephone: (914) 328-9157

A leading publisher focusing on electronic publishing, videotex, online databases, and software. It also publishes newsletters on those subjects.

>   Link Resources Corp.
>   215 Park Ave. South
>   New York, NY 10003
>   Telephone: (212) 473-5600

A research, consultancy, and publishing firm, Link details nearly every aspect of videotex, electronic publishing, online databases, video, and related subjects. It publishes the monthly *Videotex/Viewdata Report* and scores of research reports on various sectors of the electronic information industry.

>Presentation Consultants, Inc.
>2 West 45th St., Suite 1703
>New York, NY 10036
>Telephone: (212) 719-4122

An information services organization whose president, Ira Mayer, wrote *The Electronic Mailbox,* a useful book on E-mail for first-time users and businesses.

>Videotex Industry Association
>1901 N. Fort Myer Drive, Suite 200
>Rosslyn, VA 22209
>Telephone: (703) 522-0883

The VIA is the leading group supporting videotex and teletext in the United States. More than 130 companies involved in those industries receive promotion, representation, and literature from the group, which also sponsors seminars and publishes a newsletter. The VIA's Business Videotex Council deals with the experience and problems of videotex in business settings.

APPENDIX D
SELECTED SPECIALIZED DATABASES

The following databases are available through Dialog or other leading vendors. There are thousands of additional databases available. For a more complete listing and review of databases, refer to the suggested texts in the bibliography.

AGRICULTURE/FOOD

BIOSIS Previews Covers more than 9,000 journals, reviews, and reports in the biosciences.

FOODS ADLIBRA Food science and packaging information. Also covers nutrition and toxicology.

BUSINESS/ECONOMICS

Accountant's Index Articles on accounting and related professional areas.

Banker Index of articles from the daily *American Banker* newspaper.

BI/DATA Forecasts and Time Series Information on economic data from overseas countries.

BLS Series Numeric databases that cover U.S. employment, consumer prices, wages, and producer prices.

Economic Literature Index Index of journal articles, book reviews, and monographs on economics.

Harvard Business Review Online citations, abstracts, and full-text versions of the business journal.

Insurance Abstracts Covers literature on life, property, and liability insurance.

ENERGY/ENVIRONMENT

ENERGYLINE Abstracts on energy information articles.

ENVIROLINE Information on environmental law, technology, planning, and management.

GOVERNMENT/LEGISLATION

CIS A Congressional information service that covers hearings, reports, legislation, and relevant documents.

FEDREG Abstracts of the Federal Register—the government's bulletin for announcing rule changes, hearings, and laws.

GPO Monthly Catalog Index of documents produced by the legislative and executive branches.

LABORLAW Covers labor management, agreements, legislation, and administration.

LC/LINE U.S. Library of Congress documents cataloged since 1968.

Legal Resource Index Covers major law journals, newspapers, government publications, and monographs.

MEDICINE/HEALTH SCIENCES

Health Planning and Administration Nonclinical journal references on health care planning, insurance, and finance.

Medline The National Library of Medicine's index of articles from more than 3,000 domestic and international journals.

Mental Health Abstracts Citations on mental health articles, monographs, and reports.

SCIENCE / ENGINEERING / TECHNOLOGY

CLAIMS/Citation Citations on U.S. Patent Office Records and the government's patent classification system.

COMPENDEX Abstracts and references on engineering and technological subjects.

Conference Papers Index Citations from technical and scientific meetings, talks, and conferences.

INSPEC A master database that covers physics, computers, and technology.

International Software Lists software available for mini- or personal computers.

Mathfile Research information on mathematical literature worldwide.

Microcomputer Index Articles from leading publications that cover personal computer use.

NTIS A prime source of government information on research, development, and engineering being done by federal agencies.

SAE Technical papers relevant to automotive engineering and production.

SPIN References on journal articles published by American Institute of Physics. Russian articles also translated.

TRADEMARKSCAN Covers all active applications and registrations of trademarks in the U.S.

SOCIAL SCIENCES / EDUCATION

Book Review Index Covers reviews of books and periodicals published in the U.S.

Encyclopedia of Associations Information on U.S. trade, fraternal, professional, and business associations.

ERIC Covers literature on education and related areas. Compiled by National Institute of Education.

Family Resources Information on marriage, divorce, social services, education, and family services.

Foundation Directory A resource to finding more than 3,500 foundations that make grants.

Information Science Abstracts Literature on information storage and related areas.

Marquis Who's Who Biographies on more than 75,000 individuals.

NICEM Lists available nonprint educational media for educators from graduate school to preschool.

PAIS International References from journals in psychology, sociology, political science, and public administration.

Philosopher's Index Information on ethics, logic, epistemology, and metaphysics.

PsycINFO Abstracts of articles on the behavioral sciences from print version of *Psychological Abstracts*.

INDEX

ABI/INFORM, 4, 5, 59-60, 61, 98, 102, 106
Abstracts, 24, 38, 98, 102, 104, 111-112, 113, 124
ADP Automail, 142, 146
ADP Network, 42
Adtrack, 5, 109
Advertising and Marketing Intelligence (AMI), 112
After Dark, 23, 27, 59
   See also, BRS
American Business Lists, Inc., 82, 83
Area Business Databank.
   See Trade and Industry ASAP
Artificial intelligence, 7, 116, 180
ASCIT (Automated System for Consumer Information and Training), 166
Auto-dial, 34–35
Automated information transfer systems, 125
Automatic teller machines (ATMs), 160, 170
Barter Worldwide, Inc., 129
Bartering, 129–130
Batch-mode processing, 170, 176
Baud rate, 32, 34, 49, 54
Bibliographic databases, 11, 40
Bibliographic Retrieval Service. *See* BRS
BIOSIS Previews, 106
BNA Online, 113
Boolean connectors, 8
BRKTHRU, 27, 58-60, 146
   See also, BRS
BRS:
   accessing, 44
   availability of, 27, 91
   cost of, 59
   features of, 58–60

Information Access Company, 103
   as a private database, 138, 142, 146–147, 153
   research capabilities, 42, 107
   Trade and Industry ASAP, 94
Bulletin boards (electronic):
   Automail, 146
   CompuServe, 56
   definition of, 136
   Delphi, 58
   Dialcom, 153
   electronic mail, 136, 140, 146
   and private databases, 142
   The Source, 52–53
Business Arrive, 178
Business Banker, 173
Business Connection. *See* Dialog Business Connection
Business Dateline, 102–103
Business Research Corporation, 86–87
ByVideo, Inc., 165
Cableshare, 165
CACI, Inc., 5, 128
CB Simulator, 55
CBD Online, 15–16
CD players, 157, 161
CD-ROM (Compact disk read-only memory), 132-134, 155
Chase Manhattan Bank, 174–175
Citibank Direct Access, 175–176
Clusterplus, 72
Commerce Business Daily, 6, 15, 126–128
Commerce Department Trade Opportunities, 6
Communications parameters, 33
Communications software, 33
Compatibility, 168–169, 179
Competitive analysis, 14, 77, 86, 94, 95, 96, 102, 106–107, 111–112, 128
Comp-U-Card International, 161

202

CompuSave, 161
CompuServe:
　applications of, 147–149
　communications software, 33
　cost of, 23, 54
　demographics capabilities, 5, 48
　electronic mail, 6–7, 138, 141–142
　features of, 54–57, 147–149
　investment services, 90, 147
　networking, 7
　packet-switching network, 135
　popularity of, 3
　and telebanking, 177
　and Telebase systems, 39–40
　telecommunications, 9
　training, 24
　using, 117
Comp-u-store, 63
Computer Database, 113
Conferencing, 53, 55, 58, 61
　See also, Teleconferencing
Configuration, 33
Connect charges/connect time:
　BRS/BRKTHRU, 59
　CD-ROM, 133
　in choosing a database, 23
　CompuServe, 54, 148, 177
　Delphi, 57, 150
　Electronic Yellow Pages, 78
　Instant Yellow Pages, 83
　NewsNet, 64
　Nexis, 114
　and private databases, 145
　The Source, 52, 135
　in telebanking, 167
　and telebase systems, 39–40
　Videolog, 8
Consulting, 5
Conway Data, Inc., 97
Corporate intelligence, 43
Covidea, 172–174, 178–179
Credit reporting services, 64, 65, 68, 69–70, 74, 88
Customer analysis, 75
Database management, 60
Database management systems (DMS), 11
Databases:
　applications of, 4–7, 11, 73–74, 102, 110, 113, 132–180

　availability of, 27–28
　choosing, 23-25
　constructing, 7–8
　cost of, *See* individual vendors, by name
　evaluating, 45
　features of, *See* individual vendors, by name
　future of, 180
　history of, 11–12
　specialized, 15–16
　testimonials about, 13–15
　types of, 10–11
　using, 114–119
Data bits, 34
Data Courier, Inc., 102–103
Data Times, 99
Database search, 20
Delphi, 7, 57–58, 138, 149–150
Demographics, 5–6, 11, 42
　AMI, 112
　CompuServe, 48, 56, 147
　Delphi, 57
　Donnelly, 72, 74
　Dun & Bradstreet, 69
　Electronic Yellow Pages, 78
　Frost and Sullivan, 108
　Predicasts, 107
　Sitenet, 97
Dialcom, 6, 60–61, 103, 142, 149, 152–153
Dialnet, 35, 107, 117, 135
Dialog:
　availability of, 27
　Commerce Business Daily, 127
　cost of, 94
　Delphi, 57
　Dun & Bradstreet, 69
　economic data, 6
　Electronic Yellow Pages, 77
　features of, 11, 14
　International Trade Administration, 123
　Investext, 87
　Knowledge Index, 105–107
　packet-switching network, 135
　popularity of, 12
　as a research tool, 115
　SEC Reports, 90
　training, 24, 118

204 INDEX

Trinet, 96
  using, 35, 38, 42-44, 102-103, 123
Dialog Business Connection, 24, 42–44, 69, 77, 96
Digital Techniques, 165, 179
Direct mail, 13
Directories, 79–81
Disclosure, 90–91, 134
DMI (Dun & Bradstreet's Market Identifiers) 70
Dollars and Sense, 168, 174, 176
Donnelly Demographics and Marketing Information Services, 72
Dow Jones News Retrieval:
  applications of, 12, 102
  availability of, 27
  communications software, 33
  for competitive analysis, 4
  cost of, 62
  Dateline, 103
  Dialcom, 152
  for economic advice, 6, 90
  electronic mail, 48, 51
  features of, 61–64
  telebanking, 171, 176
Dumb terminals, 33
Dun & Bradstreet, 6, 43, 63, 64–76, 88, 102, 116
Dun's Decision Makers, 76
Dun's Market Identifiers, 13, 14
Dun's Marketing Services, 13, 75–76
DUNS number, 74, 103, 104, 115
DunsDial, 70
DunsPrint, 70
DunsQuest, 70
DunsVoice, 70
Duplex, 34
EasyLink, 6, 39, 129–130, 142, 151
EasyNet, 39–42, 69, 77, 117
EasyPlex, 141
ECLIPSE, 111
E-COM, 140, 149
Electronic banking, 166–180
Electronic clipping services, 60, 65, 111
Electronic filing, 146, 153
Electronic funds transfer (EFT), 167, 168–171, 174, 175, 176, 177–179
Electronic mail:
  ADP Automail, 146

availability of, 23
CompuServe, 55, 148
definition of, 48
Delphi, 58, 149
Dialcom, 60, 152
  in the electronic profit center, 6
  in private databases, 135–145
  The Source, 154–155
  in telebanking, 171–173, 175–177, 178–179
Telemail, 151
  using, 117
Videolog, 9
Electronic profit center:
  applications of, 4–7
  building, 17
  definition of, 2, 4
Electronic publishing, 144, 153, 178
Electronic reconciliation worksheet, 174
Electronic retailing, 155–166
Electronic Yellow Pages, 4, 6, 17, 44, 76–82
Electronistore, 161, 166
Engineering Literature Index, 106
Entrepreneur's Network, 56
EXCHANGE, 111
Executive information systems, 132
Excel, 176
Expert systems, 180
External databases, 11, 132
Financial screening, 43
FIND/SVP, 5
Foreign Traders Index, 6, 123–124
Frost and Sullivan Market Research Reports, 5, 59, 107, 108
Full-text databases, 11, 40
FYI News Service, 49, 129, 142
GEISCO, 150
General Electric, 142, 150–151
General Videotex Corporation, 149
Government databases, 122–128
Government regulations, 6, 42, 108, 112
Graphics, 51, 56, 141, 164
Grouplink, 58, 149–150
GTE (General Telephone and Electronics Corporation), 135, 138, 151–152
Highlights Online, 62

… INDEX   205

Industry Data Sources, 4
INFOBANK, 111–112
Infocentric:
 definition of, 2
Infocentric management strategies, 25–26
Infocentricity:
 cost of, 20–21
 growth of, 16
InfoMaster, 39–42, 69, 77
InfoPlex, 55, 147
Information Access Company, 93, 102–105, 134
Information brokers:
 cost of, 12, 29, 45, 115
 Dow Jones News Retrieval, 63
 learning from, 118
 popularity of, 16
 services of, 25, 30
 when to use, 6, 21, 69, 103, 155
Information center, 27
Information on Demand, 53
Information retrieval:
 Commerce Business Daily, 127
 Delphi, 57
 Dialog, 78
 Dun & Bradstreet, 73
 and electronic retailing, 158
 and information brokers, 29
 methods of, 39
 in private databases, 147
 The Source, 53
 in telebanking, 178, 179
Information specialists (in-house), 30–32, 48
InfoTrac, 134
INSPEC, 154
Instant Mail, 50, 51
Instant Yellow Pages, 6, 82–83
Interac Corp., 166
Interactive merchandising, 155–166
Interactive Training Systems, Inc., 166
Interactive video, 155–156
Interchange, 56, 147, 148
Interfaces, 38
Internal databases, 11
International Business Clearinghouse (IBC), 129–130

International marketing, 122–130
International Pharmaceutical Abstracts, 106
International Trade Administration (ITA), 122–126
Investext, 53–54, 86–87
Investment services:
 CompuServe, 56, 147
 Dialcom, 152
 Dow Jones News Retrieval, 63
 Electronic Yellow Pages, 79
 Investext, 86–87
 NewsNet, 64, 65
 Nexis, 111–112
 The Source, 53–54
 for telebanking, 175
I-Quest, 39–42, 55, 69, 77
JA Micropublishing, Inc., 147
Keywords, 7–8
Kingman Consulting Group, 109
Knowledge Index, 23, 24, 105–107
Laser disks, 157
Legal Resource Index, 106, 113
LegisTrak, 99
Lexis, 13, 24, 27, 110, 114
LEXPAT, 113
Libraries:
 college, 28–29
 corporate, 26–28
 online, 5
 public, 28–29, 56
Line feed, 34
List brokers, 78, 82
Listings, 11
Location analysis, 98
Lotus 1-2-3, 76, 174, 176
Magazine Index, The, 102, 104–105, 106, 113
Mail Alert, 51
Mailgrams, 52, 137, 140, 142, 152
Mailing lists, 4, 44, 73, 78, 105, 123
Management Contents, 4, 53, 59–60, 102, 104, 105, 113
Manuals, 24, 31, 49, 52, 118
 See also, Training
Manufacturers Hanover Trust (MHT), 176–177
Market analysis, 75, 77, 86, 96, 107, 111, 112, 128
Market information, 43

INDEX

Market research:
   AMI, 112
   BRS/BRKTHRU, 59–60, 147
   in choosing a database, 11
   Dun & Bradstreet, 74
   for electronic retailing, 160
   Electronic Yellow Pages, 78
   Information Access Company, 102–103
   Instant Yellow Pages, 83
   International Trade Administration, 123
   Pinpoint, 128
   in Telebase systems, 42
   Thomas Registers, 95
   Trinet, 97
Market segmentation, 75
MCI Mail, 6, 48, 50–51, 63, 137, 138, 141, 142, 148
Mead Data Central, 13, 24, 27, 35, 91, 103, 110–114, 135
Meadnet, 35, 111, 117, 135
Medis, 27, 110
Medline, 14, 106
Menu-driven systems, 38, 42, 44, 59, 117
Mergers, corporate, 5, 75, 90, 111, 112, 113, 132
MicroDisclosure, 90
Million Dollar Directory, 70–71, 116
Modem, 3, 11, 20, 21, 23, 31, 44, 139, 144, 171
   acoustic, 35
   choosing, 32
   direct-connect, 35
Moneylink, 168, 174, 176
Moody's Investor Services, 71–72, 116
Multiplan, 174
National Automated Accounting Research System (NAARS), 111
National Newspaper Index, 106, 113
Networks, 7, 53, 132, 136, 155
   See also, Private databases
New products, 4, 14, 74, 102, 106, 107, 111, 124
News services:
   AMI, 112–113
   CompuServe, 55
   Delphi, 57, 150
   Dialcom, 60–61

   Dow Jones News Retrieval, 61–62
   FYI, 59, 142
   NewsNet, 65
   Nexis, 112–113
   Predicasts, 107–108
   VU/Text, 98–99
Newsearch, 102, 105, 106, 113
NewsFlash, 65
NewsNet, 4, 5, 27, 42, 44, 64–66, 87, 88–89, 92
Nexis, 4, 11, 13, 14, 24, 27, 110–114
NTIS (National Technical Information Service), 106
Numeric databases, 11, 40
ORBIT, 44, 138, 142, 153–154
Offline prints, 24
Online libraries, 5
Oracle, 58
Packet-switching network, 35, 135–136, 145, 146, 148, 151
Paper Mail, 50
Parametric searching, 8, 10
Parity, 34
Passwords, 3, 35, 44, 52, 62, 117, 141, 176
Pergamon ORBIT Infoline, 42
PFS Plan, 176
Pinpoint, 128
Plastiserv, 148
Predicasts, 107
Private databases, 135, 138–140, 143–144
   See also, Networks
Private File, 154
Product analysis, 95
Productivity, 21, 139
Profiles, company:
   AMI, 112
   CompuServe, 56, 147
   Dow Jones News Retrieval, 63
   Dun & Bradstreet, 75
   EXCHANGE, 111
   Information Access Company, 103
   Investext, 87
   Knowledge Index, 106
   NewsNet, 65
   Nexis, 111–113
   in Telebase systems, 42
   Thomas Registers, 95
   TRW Company Profile, 65

INDEX

PROMT, 5, 59, 98, 107, 108
Prospector Research Services, Inc., 91–93
Psychographics, 72
PTS Indexes, 5, 60, 102, 107
Pulse, 34
Quick-Comm, 142, 150-151
Research and development, 5, 42
Sales leads, 13, 66, 74, 77, 80, 91, 122, 123, 125, 126
Sales prospecting:
  AMI, 112
  Business Connection, 43, 78
  Commerce Business Daily, 127–128
  databases for, 91–93
  Dun & Bradstreet, 73–75
  for the electronic profit center, 4, 13
  International Business Clearinghouse, 130
  NewsNet, 65
  Thomas Registers, 95
  Trinet, 96
Sales Prospector, 4, 65, 91–93
SalesNet, 75
Search, 27, 59
Search languages, 7–8, 38, 40, 59, 103, 106, 110, 116
Searchlink, 44–45
SEC Reports Online, 89–91
Security, 141–142
Site planning, 77, 94, 98, 111
Sitenet, 97–98
Source, The:
  accessing, 135
  cost of, 51, 135, 155
  electronic mail, 138, 142
  features of, 6, 7, 51–54, 154–155
  Investext, 87
  Management Contents, 48, 104
  teleconferencing, 142
  training, 24
Sourcemail, 52
Special interest groups (SIGs), 136
Spectrum, 174–175
Speed, 34
Spreadsheets, 3, 75, 76, 167, 168–169, 174, 176
Start-up fees, 23, 50
Stop bits, 34
Supersite, 5, 56

Supported Public Service File, 147
Symphony, 176
Synchronous, 34
Telebanking, 166–180
Telebase systems, 39–42
Telecommunications charges, 10, 12
  in choosing a database, 24
  CompuServe, 54
  Dialog, 44
  electronic mail, 145
  electronic retailing, 158, 164
  Information Access Company, 103
  Knowledge Index, 107
  Nexis, 114
  Sitenet, 97
  in telebanking, 167, 172, 173, 177
  Telemail, 152
Teleconferencing, 139, 142, 143, 150, 152
  See also, Conferencing
Telemail, 142, 151
TelemailXpress, 151
Telemarketing, 6, 68, 74, 95, 97
Telenet, 35, 107, 117, 135, 146, 147, 151–152
Telex:
  cost of, 137
  Delphi, 149
  Dialcom, 60, 152
  EasyLink, 49, 129, 142
  and electronic mail, 137, 138, 145
  future of, 180
  MCI Mail, 50
  Quick-Comm, 150
  Telemail, 151, 152
Thomas Registers, 44
  online, 94–96
Time-sharing services, 144, 148
Touchscreen, 156, 158, 161, 162–163
Trade and Industry ASAP, 93–94, 104
Trade and Industry Index, 4, 5, 102, 104, 106, 113
  See also, Trade and Industry ASAP
Trade Opportunities Program (TOP), 123
Training, 24, 31, 57, 110–111, 118, 150, 154, 155, 158, 166
  See also, Manuals

Travel services:
  Business Connection, 43
  CompuServe, 54–55, 147
  Delphi, 150
  Dialcom, 60, 152
  Dow Jones News Retrieval, 63
  Dun & Bradstreet, 69, 72–73
  NewsNet, 65
Trends analysis, 102, 112
Trinet, 96–97
TRW credit reports, 64, 88–89
Tymnet, 35, 107, 117, 135, 146, 147
Tymshare, 135
Uninet, 107, 117, 147
User guides. *See,* Manuals

User-friendly systems, 8, 38, 44, 156
Utilities, online, 48–66
Value-added information, 2
Video Financial Services, 177
Videolog, 8–10
Videotex, 3, 9, 135, 143, 171
Volume discounts, 49, 50, 153
VU/Quote, 64, 98
VU/Text, 42, 44, 91, 98–99, 103
WATS, 146
Western Union, 6, 39, 40, 48, 129–130, 137, 138, 142
Word processing, 152, 180
WPMail, 152